TWILL BASKETRY

A Handbook of Designs, Techniques, and Styles

TWILL BASKETRY

A Handbook of Designs, Techniques, and Styles

• Shereen LaPlantz •

Lark Books

1993 by Lark Books
reet
rth Carolina, U.S.A., 28801

nereen LaPlantz

Dierks
a Montgomery
laine Thompson, Sandra Montgomery, Geri Camarda

74-64-X

ngress Cataloging-in-Publication Data
reen
ketry : a handbook of designs, techniques, and styles / Shereen LaPlantz.
    cm.
bibliographical references and index.
37274-64-X
t making.   2. Twill.   I. Title.
    1992
0   92-29051
                                                          CIP

5 4 3 2 1

as been made to ensure that all information in this book is accurate. However, due to
itions, tools, and individual skills, the publisher cannot be responsible for any injuries,
er damages which may result from the use of the information in this book.

ng Kong by Oceanic Graphic Printing.

: Anonymous, Tarahumara, Mexico. Double-woven twill. Pine needles and palm.
ction of Kathy Dannerbeck.

Acknowledgements

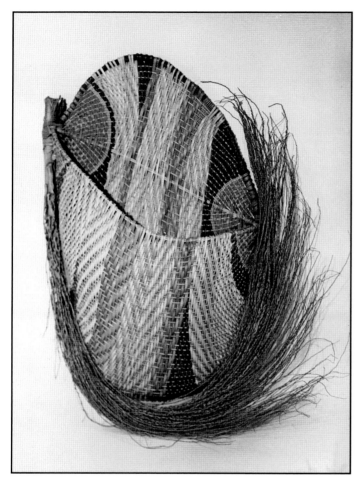

DEDICATION:

To Jim Widess, who suggested this book and always sends exciting thoughts, information, and photos; and to Betty Kemink, an innovative artist and teacher, who asked the question that convinced me to write this book.

Left: "South Wind" by Betty Kemink. Twill weave on rib-construction basket. Palm seed stem, grapevine, dyed reed, 24" x 35" x 6", 1991.

Below: Anonymous, backpack, Borneo. Photo: © James B. Widess.

ACKNOWLEDGEMENTS:

Obviously, many people helped with this project, but special thanks go out to some special people. Sherry O'Conner proofed the manuscript by making each one of the baskets. A group of exciting women who took my workshop in Seattle exposed me to many new ideas about color. Pam Niemi, who was traveling and studing in Guatemala, bought many of the basket examples. Judy Mulford sent me photographs of her collection, and, to get me going, Irene Gettle sent me dyed reed. My husband, David, who encourages all of my projects, helped this time with photography and many meals.

My heartfelt gratitude goes to Virginia Hoffman, my first weaving teacher at Los Angeles State. One day she took an hour to teach me the concepts behind the patterns, and how to design and draft my own patterns. This book would not have been possible without that hour.

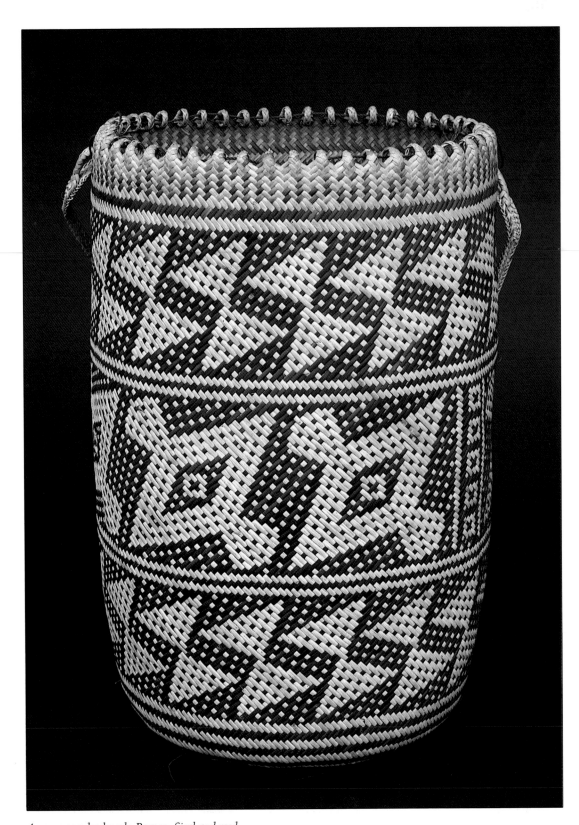

Anonymous, backpack, Borneo. Sisal and reed.

Table of Contents

My favorite teaching and learning experiences are when I can sit next to someone, and we weave baskets together. Slowly, gently we share our knowledge of the techniques and the character of those techniques.

Let's take the time to go slowly. Come, sit with me. We'll make baskets together and talk about twill.

"Round Mulberry Basket" by Dorothy Gill Barnes. 12" x 9" x 11", 1987. Photo: Doug Martin. From the collection of the Karl Road Library, Columbus, Ohio.

What is Twill?

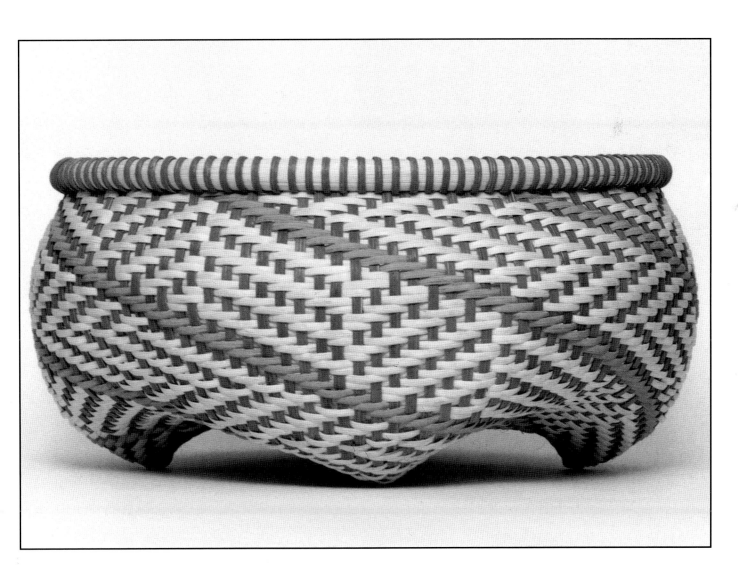

"Helter-Skelter" by Judith Olney. Stepped twill derived from a Maori design. Reed, 7" x 15" dia., 1991. Photo: Roger Olney.

We see twills most often in fabrics. Twills can be identified by an overall diagonal pattern in the weave. Jeans frequently are twill. Herringbone and hound's tooth jackets are also twills.

Twill fabrics are flat; therefore, they can only start at one end and go to the other. Baskets are magical. They're dimensional. In basketry, twills can wrap around edges and corners!

Let's start with the basics. Plain weave is an over one, under one pattern. Twill's diagonal pattern is created by weaving over or under more than one, and starting each new row one step over from the last. The illustrations help make it obvious.

Weaving over three, under one, as shown in the first illustration, creates an "unbalanced twill." Unbalanced twills have a visually stronger diagonal line but are not as sturdy. Tension in an unbalanced weave can also be a problem.

The second illustration shows a balanced twill. It weaves over and under the same number of elements, like over two, under two, or over three, under three. These twills are sturdier, and the tension is easier to handle.

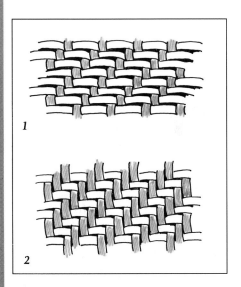

Right top: "A Nantucket Twill" by Carol and Dick Lasnier. Nantucket lightship basket. Walnut, cane, ivory, 13" x 11" dia., 1991.

Bottom: "Lightning" by Sosse Baker. A 1/1/1/4 continuous twill. Dyed and natural flat oval reed, 22" x 22" x 22", 1991. Photo: Sosse Baker.

Actually, the differences between balanced and unbalanced twills are minimal. In general, twills create a strong, sturdy fabric or basket. Choose which twill to use based on aesthetics or which ones interest you. There is one exception to this broad invitation: large, functional baskets that must carry heavy loads, like laundry baskets, must be woven from a balanced twill. Over two, under two is usually the best twill for these baskets.

Now let's look at some twill baskets and explore the possibilities. Twills can form a series of continuous diagonal lines spiraling up the side of the basket.

For design purposes, the diagonal lines can also make zigzag patterns. These zigzags can switch back and forth whenever you wish.

The vertical zigzags of the Tarahumara basket are smaller and less prominent than those in Sosse Baker's "Lightning." Take note of the horizontal lines around the Tarahumara basket's neck; they indicate that this is a bias plaited basket.

Twills can also be interspersed with plain weave. In "Quilting Basket," single lines of twill spiral through the plain weave.

Top: "Quilting Basket" by Jeanmarie Mako and David Blaisus. Oak, 16" x 10" x 12", 1991. Photo: Rick Green.

Bottom: Anonymous, Tarahumara tribe of northern Mexico. Double layer, 2/2 twill. Pine needle and palm, 4" x 4-1/2" dia., contemporary. Photo: David LaPlantz. From the collection of Jennifer Rice.

Above: Anonymous, Guatemala. A 2/2 twill with 2-block patterns. Palm, 4" x 3" dia., contemporary. Photo: David LaPlantz. Collected by Pam Niemi.

Right: Untitled by Judith Olney. Double quatrefoil. Reed, 10" x 10" dia., 1990. Photo: Roger Olney.

Below: "Victorian Laundry Basket" by Joyce Schaum. Rattan reed with white oak handles, 24" x 24" x 17", 1991. Photo: Gary Schaum.

Opposite page, top: Untitled by Lyn Siler. Rattan, 10" x 5" x 13", 1991. Photo: Will Siler.

Opposite bottom: "Victorian Basket" by Joyce Schaum. Rattan reed, 13" x 13" x 11", 1990. Photo: Gary Schaum.

If twill diagonals can make zigzags running up the basket, then they can also make zigzags running around the basket. Judith Olney uses up-and-down points (like a herringbone fabric) that are designed to accentuate the pointed feet. The design also incorporates a wide band of plain weave.

If you work some of the zigzags upside down and some right side up, then you get diamonds. Joyce Schaum's twill diamonds are juxtaposed with diamond-shaped spaces of plain weave. Zigzags are again used to accentuate the corners of the base.

The diamonds can be elaborated. In Lyn Siler's basket, several types of lines form diamonds with exaggerated shapes. Notice that the complex twills are woven in a band around the basket. It is possible to develop a twill in the base and wrap the same twill up the sides, but it is by no means a requirement to do so.

Below: Anonymous, lidded basket, Philippines. Bamboo with beaded handle, 4" x 4" x 7", old.

Right: "Oh Why?" by Zoe Morrow. Twill and plain weave. Shredded money, 6" x 7-1/4" x 1-3/4", 1991. Photo: Charles H. Jenkins III.

Finally, twills can become as complex as you wish. The title of Zoe Morrow's piece is "Oh Why?", and you can see the letters "O" and "Y" on the basket.

As we sit here together working on twills, we'll walk through the basics, developing a thorough foundation. Then we'll look at how to create your own twills by combining variations and by designing your own weaves. There is, essentially, no limit to what you can design. We'll even work on an alphabet, so you can write poetry through the weave of your basket.

Along the way, we'll examine the impact of color. Color is such a strong element that it can obliterate the weave pattern, or you can develop one pattern in the weave and another, complementary pattern in the color.

Finally, we'll touch on shaping. Only a few possibilities are included since this is a twill book, not a shaping book, but you don't need to feel restricted. Apply twills to all of your favorite shapes. They will work, even on stair-step pyramids!

Wrapping Up the Sides

T wills can be worked any number of ways on a basket. They can form a band all the way around, a spot on a side or base, or they can start on the base and wrap up the basket.

"Kobokurin" (ancient tree rings) by Jiro Yonezawa. Bamboo, cedar root, and cane, 10" x 7-1/2" dia. Photo: Toshihiko Shibata.

Wrapping Up the Sides

First, let's remember that you don't need to, and may not wish to, wrap the same twill up the sides that you use in the base. Consider what type of basket you want, and what type of design would enhance it best. There are many beautiful options.

Starting with the traditional, wooden base, this Nantucket basket (right) uses plain weave for a few beginning rows. The twill starts after the sides have been established. Notice that the light weavers form the twill by floating over three stakes.

This bag (below) is common throughout the South Pacific. It is made from a single palm frond—the leaves are plaited together, away from the center spine. It's finished by braiding all the ends together into a three-strand (pigtail) braid for the base. The center spine stays at the top, and it is split to open up the top of the basket. Since this basket is woven from top to bottom, the base cannot set up the weave. Many of the more complex twills from the people of the South Pacific Islands and the Maori (New Zealand) are

Above: "A Nantucket Twill" by Carol and Dick Lasnier. Nantucket lightship basket with a 1/1/1/3 twill. Walnut, cane, ivory, 13" x 11" dia., 1991. Photo: Carol Lasnier.

Left: Anonymous, from Belau, Micronesia. Coconut frond, 16-1/2" x 11" x 10", 1978. Photo: Judy Mulford. From the collection of Judy Mulford.

either woven top to bottom, or woven flat and made into a tube. These are all finished with a three-strand braid at the bottom, seaming the two sides together.

If you wish to wrap the twill up the sides of your basket, you must start in the center and work outward.

Think of the basket base as having quadrants, and work toward the outer corner of each quadrant. There are two basic types of twills: diamonds and blocks. The illustrations show how to build outward with each basic twill. As you can see, the square base stops some of the diagonal lines. Those diagonals continue to meet

*"Indian Quilt" by Joan Moore. Black ash, 2-3/4" x 2-3/4" x 2-1/2", 1989.
Photo: Dick Moore.*

and form points as the sides build.

All of this will be shown again in the step-by-step directions. Just remember, the trick to wrapping any twill up the sides of your basket is to start in the center, think quadrants, and work outward.

These double-layer nesting baskets (below) begin inside on the base, weave up, turn a rim, allow a long outside rim float for decoration, weave down the sides, and finish on the outside in the base. The twill pattern begun in the original base continues throughout each of these baskets, repeating itself for the final base.

*Anonymous, Tarahumara nested baskets from Chihuahua, Mexico. Yucca, 9" x 17" dia., 1989.
Photo: Judy Mulford. From the collection of Judy Mulford.*

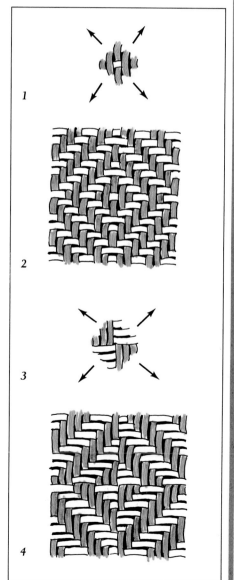

1

2

3

4

Any materials you normally use for plaiting or weaving baskets work well for twills, but flat materials are the best for showing off the pattern. Slightly domed materials, like flat oval reed, give a sturdier, more solid appearance while still showing off the pattern.

Stiffer materials, like hardwood splints, allow the floats to be longer before they snag on things. Floats are the "overs" in your pattern. They run both horizontally and vertically since baskets can be turned in any direction.

Imagine the difference between a hardwood basket and a ribbon basket. You can easily visualize the ribbon basket snagging or catching on things. In contrast, it is difficult to imagine the hardwood basket catching on anything unless it has a long, sloppy float.

Flexible materials are needed for bias plaiting and any of the more complex shapes. It is possible to bias plait with stiff materials; it's just not as much fun.

Some materials suitable for twill include: reed, river cane, binding cane, bamboo, hardwood splints, microwood (a thin hardwood veneer on a Kraft paper backing), palm blades, pink palm, New Zealand flax, ribbon, paper (especially the heavier papers like cover stock, heavy watercolor papers, or handmade papers), lauhala, braided bamboo, braided straw, and braided smoked buri.

Cattails compress too much to plait nicely. Dracaena and yucca taper too quickly, but can be cut into precise strips if you wish to use them.

TIP: If you're using something that must be cut into strips, like microwood or paper, a pasta cutter makes a 5-inch grouping of 1/4-inch strips quickly. Think fettucini. Rug cutting and leather cutting devices also work.

MEASURING YOUR MATERIALS

Measure the length to cut each element as you would for any plaited basket. I recommend taking a piece of your material, making a "U" the size of the desired basket, adding on for the rim, and cutting.

Estimate the number of elements to cut by measuring the desired size of your base and dividing the width of your elements into it. Twill elements actually slip in close to each other, so simple math works. For example, for a 6-inch by 6-inch base of 1/4-inch-wide strips, multiply 6 x 4 = 24. Then double 24, because the elements weave in two directions.

The exact dimensions of your base, and the total number of elements, will also be affected by the fact that each twill has an increment. The increment is the number by which a twill grows naturally. Let me emphasize this. If you consistently use the appropriate increments, your twills will have complete (versus incomplete) patterns. Most twills also have a "center unit," a pattern in the center, that doesn't repeat.

Anonymous, quiver. A 2/2 twill. Bamboo, 26" x 3-1/2" dia., contemporary. Photo: David LaPlantz. From the collection of David and Shreen LaPlantz.

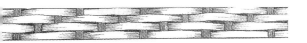

Tension and Color Tips

"Tribute to Cornelia French" by Susi Nuss, interior. Black ash and shagbark hickory, 4" x 10" dia., 1988. Photo: Susi Nuss.

Before getting into the patterns and weaving techniques, you need to be aware of a couple of areas where twills add complications to your basketry. Tension is always a primary concern for good

Tension and Color

craftsmanship, and color sets off the patterns to their full beauty; with twills, both can be troublesome without some advance preparation.

TENSION TROUBLES

The tension for twills is a "plaited" tension, one that is equal in all directions. There is a natural tendency to pack tightly in one direction. Try to get all of the elements evenly spaced and the tension equidistant in all directions.

The tension in the first illustration is even; all of the elements are uniformly spaced in all directions. The equal spacing highlights the twill patterns.

The second illustration is an example of "woven" tension. Notice how one set of elements is widely spaced, while the others are packed tightly. This type of tension distorts the twill patterns. In fact, this illustration seriously distorts its own 2-block twill.

It's easiest to get an even tension if you start in the center and work outward. Remember, you have to start in the center and work outward to get the twills to wrap up the sides and around corners.

Start with the center unit. Illustration 3 shows a 2-block twill (explained in detail in the "Basic Blocks" chapter), so the center unit is four elements across four elements.

With a 2-block twill, the enlarging increment is two. Add two elements to each of the four sides. Adjust the tension, making everything even. By working this way, the tension is easy to adjust; it's almost automatic. (Refer to illustrations 4 through 7.)

Continue adding two elements to each of the four sides, as shown in illustration 8, until the base is the desired size. Adjust the tension as you go.

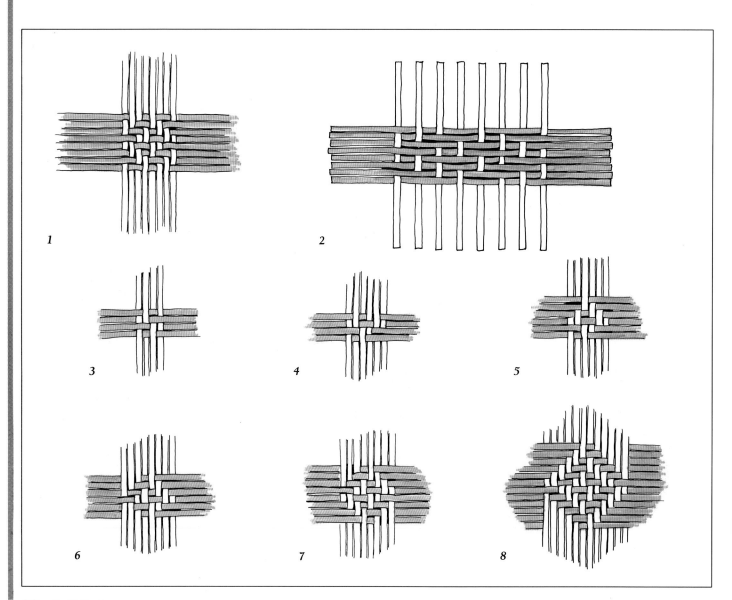

An Alternative Weaving Method

The other way to weave twills is to set up a warp. Align all of the elements in one direction (usually vertically); then weave each new element all the way across. (See illustration 9.) The natural tendency using this method is for the verticals to be too close together. Getting an even tension can be difficult.

TIP: Weave the entire base loosely; then adjust the tension from the center outward, working in increments. Illustration 10 shows how the loose weave looks before the tension has been adjusted.

With two styles of weaving, when do you choose one style over the other? Weaving from the center outward works best for basic twills or when you're designing as you weave. Setting up a warp and weaving across it is a better method when working with a draft (a pattern on graph paper). Since the draft shows the complete pattern for each row, it's easier to weave an entire row before starting the next row. You'll be using drafts for complex twills and for your own designs.

Scalloping Tension

Floats can cause tension problems, and all twills have floats. Sometimes elements can slip under floats and, by not taking up their allotted space, those elements can cause the tension to get too tight. As you're weaving, constantly check the tension. Make sure everything is even and uses its full space, but no extra space.

You may find it easier to get an evenly spaced tension by weaving two or three rows all at one time. For example, when you upstake, turn up the sides and weave one row across a side, then the second row across that same side, then the third row before going to the next side. Although it's technically possible to weave each row singly, the tension is much harder to master that way.

The side view of the sample basket (below) shows the elements slipping under floats and scalloping with tension that is

Left: Untitled sample by author, interior. Block twill variation. Micro-wood, 7" x 7" x 4", 1990. Photo: author.

Below: Untitled sample by author, detail.

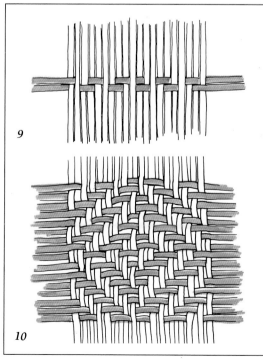

9

10

Untitled sample by author. A 3-block twill. Microwood, 9" x 9" x 4", 1991. Photo: author.

Untitled sample by Sherry O'Connor. A 1-block (or broken-diamond) twill. Reed, 3" x 3" x 5-3/4", 1991. Photo: author.

Untitled by Tom Colvin. Louisiana Choctaw-style, shallow bowls in various twills. River cane, smallest: 6" dia., early 1980's.

Anonymous,
Guatemala.
A 3-block base
for a 2/2 twill.
Palm, 4-1/2" x
4" dia., contem-
porary. Photo:
David LaPlantz.
Collected by
Pam Niemi.

Guatemalan
basket,
another
view.

too tight. This basket also shows how to turn bad tension to your advantage. With the sides too tight, the rim was flared, creating an interesting shape.

Plain weave takes up more space than twill. That's a tension difference you can use as a design tool. In the sample basket, three rows of plain weave were added at the top, flaring out the rim. Another row or two of plain weave would have flared the rim more, any additional rows would continue to build up the sides, but with a bulge.

COLOR

Color can be used very dramatically with twill patterns, as you'll see later in the "Color" chapter. For now you need to know that color adds complication imme- diately, to every twill basket. In addition, the effects of color in bias plaiting are radically different from those seen in straight plaiting.

Straight Plaiting

When straight plaiting, the easiest way to show off the twill pattern is to use three colors. Choose one for each of the two directions in the base, and select a third color for around the sides.

Using one color for the sides and one for the base results in a solid base, obscur- ing both the pattern and how the pattern wraps up the sides. If you chose two col- ors for the base and repeat one on the sides, then two of the sides are obscured instead.

Bias Plaiting

In bias plaiting, the sides divide in half, and the halves weave across each other. Therefore, working two colors in the base, one for each direction, results in a plaid basket.

If you want one color in each direction for the sides, the elements must be dyed, stained, or somehow colored. Each ele- ment must be one color for half and another color for the other half (see illus- tration 11). This is called space dyeing.

Next they must be arranged in rota- tion, as shown in illustration 12. This way, both the base and the sides have a solid color in each direction, which high- lights the twill pattern.

Note: The dyed or stained edges will probably be irregular, as illustrated. Since

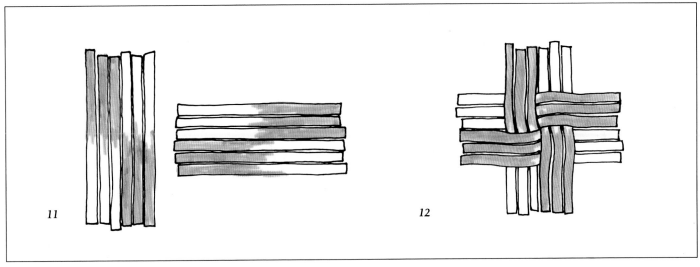

11

12

Anonymous, Philippine lidded basket. Twill with overlay. Bamboo, 12" x 12" x 14", old. From the collection of Nora Smids.

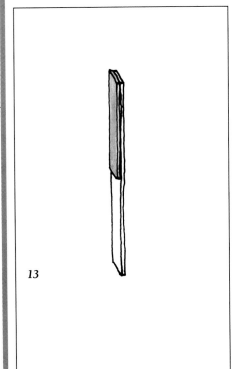

13

14

it's very hard to get a straight, even color change, accept the irregularity as part of the aesthetics of your baskets.

If you don't want to bother with space dyeing the elements, try making a plaid. It can be quite lovely, although it does obscure the twill.

Overlay

Dyes and stains are toxic, and you need to wear good rubber gloves and splash goggles when working with them. When working with the powders, wearing a mask is a necessity. In addition, you must be careful about how you dispose of any dyes and stains (check with your local EPA for disposal guidelines).

You can get around all the problems of toxicity by using an overlay. Simply lay another element over your original one. (To emphasize this, the elements in illustration 13 are as thick as boards. Basketry elements are thinner, of course.)

Overlay allows you to place a color precisely where you want it, as shown in illustration 14, and the sides can be any color you wish. Obviously, this won't work if you're using thick materials, like half round reed. It works best with something completely flat, such as microwood, palm blades, or flat reed.

Overlay can also be a design highlight. In this example from the Philippines, it is used to draw your eye to specific parts of the basket. Imagine using overlay to emphasize one section of twill or to pull the viewer's eye around the basket.

Basic Diamonds

To make a diamond, you need points on all four corners; therefore, you must use an odd number of elements. That means diamonds are limited to straight plaiting. In bias plaiting, you must have an even

"Diamond Back" by Zoe Morrow, back view. Plain weave and twill. Shredded money, 6" x 8" x 1-1/2", 1991. Photo: Charles H. Jenkins III.

number of elements, because you divide a side in half and weave the two halves across each other.

As mentioned previously, each twill has an increment, and most have a center unit. For each pattern described in this and the following chapters, increment numbers and center units are specified along with the step-by-step instructions.

WARNING: If you have never straight- or bias-plaited a basket, go the "Basic Plaiting" appendix and practice plaiting before trying to make twills. Twill is not a beginning technique.

Measure the length to cut each element, and determine the number of elements you need for your sample basket. Then let's start making some diamonds!

THE BASIC DIAMOND

Increment: This basic diamond pattern has an increment of two, with a center unit of five (i.e., five horizontal and five vertical elements). This is an over two, under two, or a 2/2 twill.

Right: "Diamond Back" by Zoe Morrow, front view.

Below: Untitled sample by Sherry O'Connor. A 2/2 diamond twill. Watercolor paper, 4-1/2" x 4-1/2" x 3-1/2", 1991. Photo: David LaPlantz.

Start weaving the center of the base with five elements (see illustration 1). If you find it difficult to control five loose elements, secure them to your work table with masking tape or clamps.

With a new, separate element, weave under two, over one, under two across the center (illustration 2).

Using two more elements on both sides of the center, weave over one, under three, over one (illustration 3).

Again add two elements to each side of the center. Weave over two, under one, over two, as shown in illustration 4, and adjust the tension so that it's even all around. You've just completed the center unit. Do you see a diamond? That's what you want.

Notice that at the points of the diamond, you weave one row under three and the next row under one. To continue, you weave the next row over three and the following row over one. Make sure that the points are always under three, under one, over three, over one. (They can also be over three, over one, under three, under one. It's the three-one pattern that's critical.) The three-one point pattern also sets up the necessary "stepping" for the overall diagonal pattern.

Away from the points, this is an under-two, over-two twill. In fact, most of the time you'll be counting in "two's." (There are a lot of partially finished rows right now, but don't be concerned with them.)

Enlarge by adding increments of two. The first row above the center unit is under one, over three, under one (illustration 5).

Add the second element above the center unit by weaving under two, over one, under two (illustration 6).

As shown in illustration 7, weave in two additional elements below, just as you did above.

Now add two elements on one side. For the first row, weave over everything until you get to the center; then weave under three and over everything else. In the next row, weave over everything until you get to the center; then weave under one and over everything else. Refer to illustration 8.

On the other side, add two elements and weave them the same way (see illustration 9). Even up the tension all around. The diamond is growing.

Add two more rows to each of the four

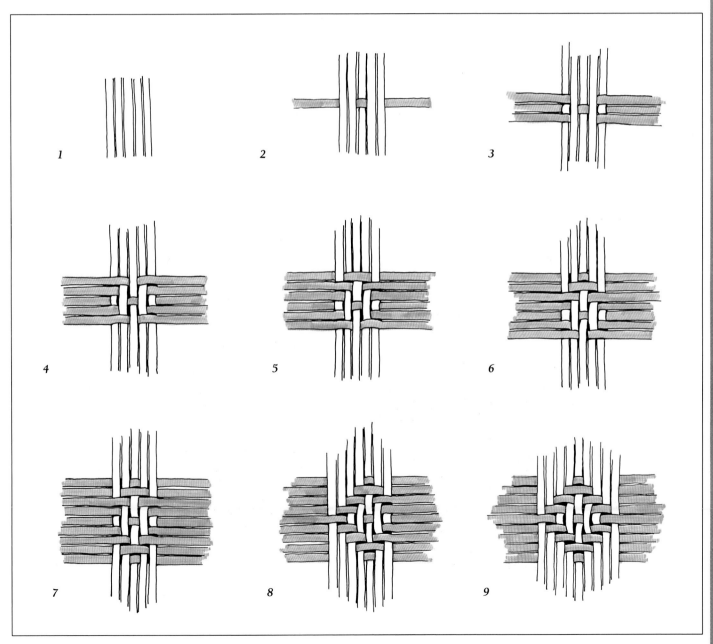

10

must weave across the points first. Weave under three, then under one, for the top and bottom; weave over three, then over one, on the sides. Adjust the tension and examine your diamond. The results so far should look like a diamond.

By the way, I'm not telling you precisely what to weave on each row (i.e., row 1: under 2, over 2, under 2, over 1, under 2, over 2, under 2), because I want you to learn how to build a pattern and keep to that pattern. If you get used to row-by-row instructions, you'll be married to those instructions and need new ones for every new twill you try. If you can look at a pattern and understand how it grows, then you can develop your own twills.

Add two more rows on each side (illustration 11). This time the horizontal elements weave over two and under everything else, but again the points are three and one. Before going further, make sure that the tension is even. Continue adding more rows, two to each side, until the dia-

mond's points reach the size you want for the base. Adjust the tension after adding each set of rows. Use clothespins or other clips to hold everything in place.

TIP: As of this writing, Radio Shack offers extremely small "micro clips." These are smooth-jawed, despite the fact they may be called "alligator" clips. They're not cheap, but they are stronger than clothespins. They can also hold everything in place without interfering with the weaving.

When the diamond is the desired size, fill in the corners with the twill pattern of over two and under two. (Illustration 12 shows the completed base.) Check and adjust the tension as you work.

With the completion of the square, you now have your base. Is it what you want? If not, now is the time to add more elements if it's too small, or take out some if it's too big. If it's askew, adjust the tension. This is the base as it will be forever. Make it wonderful!

sides, as shown in illustration 10. Most of this is simply weaving the existing verticals over two, then under everything else. Remember, the elements you're adding

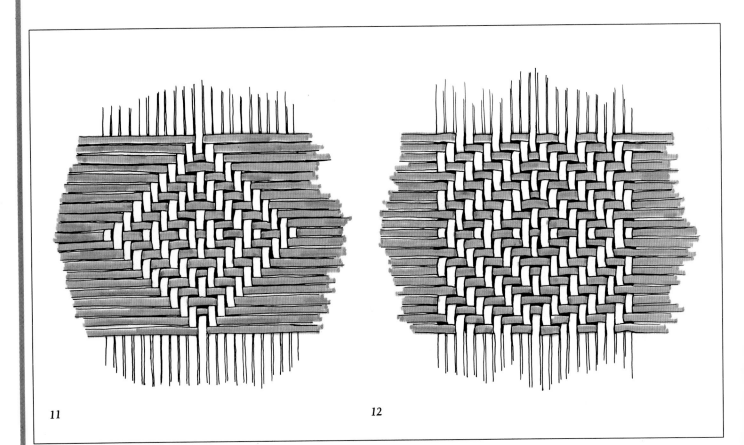

11   12

An Alternative Weaving Method

Instead of starting in the middle and building outward, you may find it easier to set up a warp. This many loose elements are almost impossible to control without securing all of them at one end. Fix one set of ends with a clamp, clipboard clip, books, or masking tape. If you're using ribbon, pins might work, but usually masking tape or a clamp is more effective.

Make sure they are all laying right next to each other, allowing for tight, but even tension.

Start in the center of the base. Weave a row across in the over two, under two pattern until you reach the center element. There, weave over one, then continue the over two, under two pattern until you reach the edge. Illustration 13 shows the complete row. You may find it easier to start in the center and weave outward to each side.

Weave a row above and below the center row, following the twill pattern (illustration 14). If the first row was "over one" at the center, then the adjacent rows will be "under three" at the center.

Add another row on each side of what you've already woven. The center of these new rows is now "under one." (Refer to illustration 15.)

Continue adding elements on each side of what you've woven, and maintain the twill pattern. (See illustration 16.) Stop when you have a square base.

Now comes the ticklish part. With this method, the warp tends to be very close together, and the weavers (weft) cannot weave in as tightly. That creates an uneven tension. The results are better if you weave the base loosely, then tighten it from the center outward to get an even tension. Check the earlier section on tension for more detailed directions.

The Sides

There is no special trick to starting the sides; use the same techniques as you would for any plaited basket. Upstake (i.e., fold all of the elements up around the base's edge) and, using a new ele-

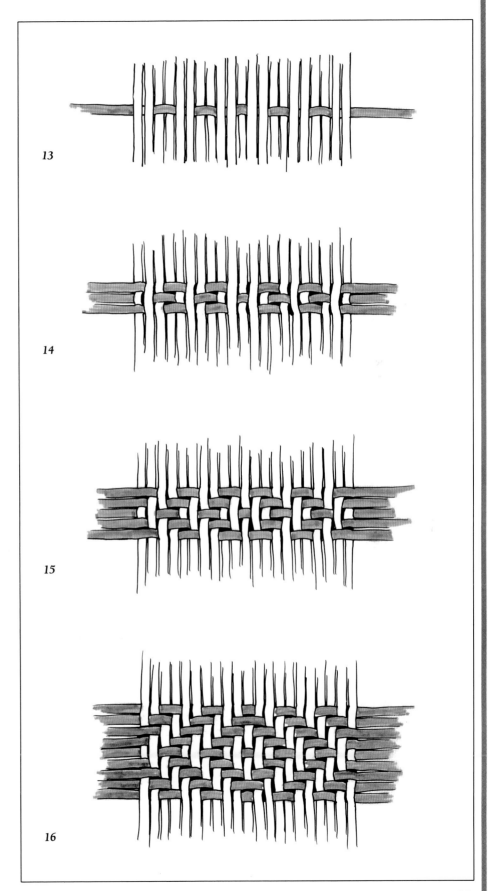

13

14

15

16

Untitled sample by author. A 2/2 diamond twill. Microwood, 5-1/2" x 5-1/2" x 6", 1992. Photo: David LaPlantz.

As demonstrated in illustration 17, be sure to continue the twill pattern. As you weave in the first row, keep checking the base to make sure you are maintaining the twill pattern. There are still four points on the diamond, and now those points are in the center of each side.

Weave in a second row, again continuing the twill pattern. Illustration 18 shows how the twill wraps up from the base onto the side. That's the excitement of twills.

TIP: As mentioned earlier, I find it easier to get an even tension if I weave the first three rows up the side together, chasing style. That means, weave one row across a side, then the second, and the third, then go to the next side. Slightly stagger the beginnings so that all of the overlapping ends aren't at the exact same spot.

There is another reason for weaving three rows at once: it sets up the twill pattern for the sides, reducing the number of times you have to check the base to confirm the pattern. All of the rest of the rows can build off the first three.

Trick–Problem–Trick

WARNING: The pattern is NOT CONTINUOUS around the corners! You haven't made an error; it's a "pattern break." This is an invisible line in the weave that causes a mirror image. If the row weaves over one before the pattern break, it changes to under one after. If it's under two before, then it's over two after.

Illustrations 19 and 20 show a pattern break. The first shows it where it occurs at the corner. The other opens it out flat, so it's easier to see.

Be careful—it's easy to weave along, chanting the rhythm of the twill, and forget the pattern break. Part way along the next side, you'll notice the twill has gone wrong. If that happens, go back to the pattern break and re-weave from there.

One final warning: on an over two, under two twill, every other row works at the pattern break. Specifically, at the pattern break, one row is under two, over one, under one, over two. The next row is under two, over two, under two, over two. The regular pattern works, and is its own mirror image, for every other row.

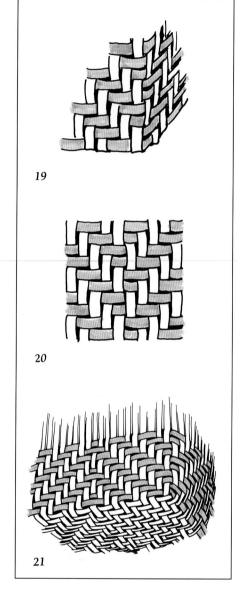

19

20

21

Keeping the pattern break in mind, weave up the sides. Maintain your twill pattern throughout, as shown in illustration 21. When your basket is the desired height, finish off the ends by making a rim. If you don't have a favorite rim, try one from the "Basic Plaiting" appendix.

VARIATION– DIAMONDS ON THE SIDES

You don't have to keep your basket totally simple. You can make diamonds on each side as well as on the base. Diamonds, herringbone, and even irregu-

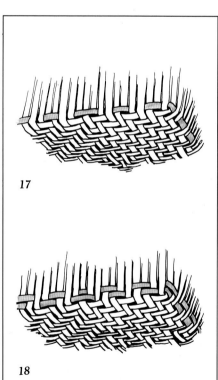

17

18

ment, weave a row around the basket. Overlap the ends and clip off the excess. Start each new row with another element. Stagger the starting points; you don't want all of the overlapping ends to fall in the same location.

Untitled sample by author. A 2/2 diamond twill. Microwood, 5-1/2" x 5-1/2" x 7", 1992. Photo: David LaPlantz.

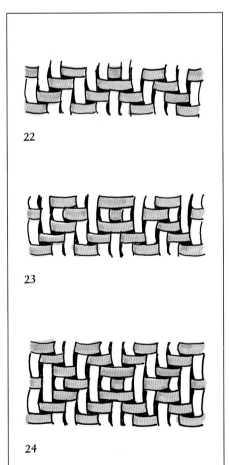

22

23

24

lar zigzags are created by reversing direction wherever you wish.

Start at one of the diamond's points, as shown in illustration 22. (The point is where the pattern comes to a "one;" whether it weaves over one or under one doesn't matter.)

Reverse direction by repeating the last "three" row (in illustration 23, it's an over three row).

As shown in illustration 24, continue weaving the twill pattern in the new direction. Just repeat this process every time you wish to change direction.

VARIATION– SOLID CENTER

You don't have to have an over one "polka dot" in the center of your diamond. You can make a solid center instead. This works best if you're using narrow elements; otherwise, the float can get too long.

Skip the over one part of the first row, and weave under all five center elements (see illustration 25). Then continue just like you did in the first twill pattern (illustration 26).

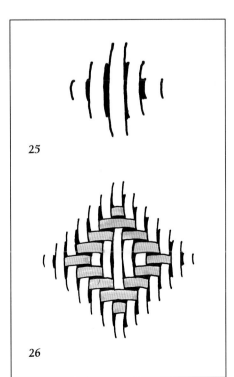

25

26

Untitled sample by author. A plus mark, diamond twill. Flat reed, 6-1/2" x 6-1/2" x 3-1/2", 1992. Photo: David LaPlantz.

VARIATION– PLUS MARK CENTER

The center diamond can be reduced in size to a plus mark.

Increment: This variation has an increment of two and a center unit of three (in each direction).

As shown in illustration 27, start by weaving the center unit, three elements across three elements. The center row is over three, and the rows on each side are under one, over one, under one.

This center unit is the only new or different part of this twill. From now on, it's an over two, under two twill, just like the basic diamond.

Add two elements on each of the four sides (illustration 28). Since this is a diamond pattern, the points still follow the three, one routine.

Add more elements, two rows to each side, until the diamond is the desired size. Illustration 29 shows how this diamond develops. Adjust the tension after weaving each set of rows.

Fill in the corners as shown in illustration 30, maintaining the twill pattern. Then adjust the tension in the corners.

Upstake and weave the sides, continuing the pattern set up by the base (illustration 31). Finish off with your favorite rim.

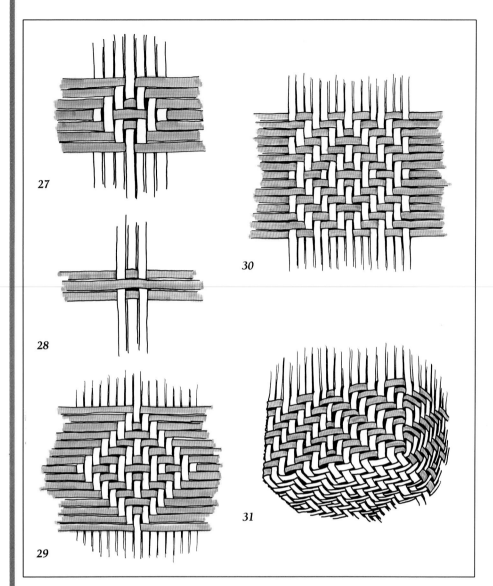

27

28

29

30

31

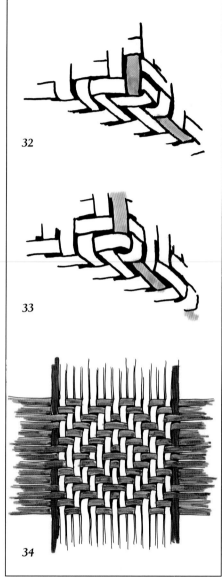

32

33

34

Beware–Problem–Beware

Sometimes a twill pattern will not automatically weave perfect corners. Many tribal peoples don't worry about this problem and just weave whatever corner develops. Their baskets are beautiful and extremely functional, but I prefer to make a solid corner.

You can see that the corner in illustration 32 locks each element in place. Nothing slides around, because the weave holds each corner element firmly. The highlighted edge element weaves under the last base element and over the first side row. The under/over locks it in place. (An over/under works equally well, of course).

Look carefully at the corner in illustration 33 Notice how the highlighted element weaves under the last base element and under the first side row. By weaving under (or over) those two elements, the element on the edge can slip around inside the basket.

Because I don't like a sloppy corner, I adjust the base. Just add two elements, one each to two opposite sides. (Refer to illustration 34.) It doesn't matter which two sides, as long as they're opposite. This alters the twill a bit (two sides will be

one row further along in the pattern). It also makes the base slightly rectangular, but I prefer this to a sloppy corner. The choice is yours. As I said, many choose to have the base square and the twill perfect, so they put up with the sloppy corners.

Always check your corners before upstaking to see if they'll work out all right. If they don't, decide then whether or not to add more elements to guarantee a solid corner.

TIP: The corners on basic diamonds tend to be fine; plus mark diamonds need adjustment. Diamond variations can work out either way.

VARIATION—
RECTANGLES

Rectangles can be made out of any diamond (or any twill). The easiest way to make a rectangle is to stop weaving before the base makes a square (illustration 35). Once the base is the size and proportion you wish, upstake and weave around the sides. Finish off with your favorite rim.

Another type of rectangle actually alters the twill pattern. If the center diamond is repeated, but in only one direction, then you have a rectangle.

Start by making a basic diamond, five elements across five elements. Add

Untitled sample by author. A 2/2 diamond twill. Microwood, 10-1/4" x 6-1/4" x 3-3/4", 1992. Photo: David LaPlantz.

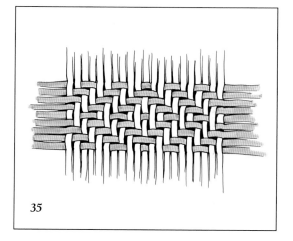

35

Anonymous, oriental. A 2/2 diamond twill. Bamboo, 12" x 18" x 4", contemporary. From the collection of Joanne Harris.

a second diamond just below it, making sure they share the same point. To do so, add only four elements to make the center unit for the second diamond. Refer to illustration 36 for guidance. When the second diamond is complete, adjust the tension.

Add two elements to each of the four sides, and maintain the twill pattern (see illustration 37). Continue adding elements until the base is the desired size. As you weave, remember to adjust the tension after each set of additional elements.

Weave in the corners as shown in illustration 38; then upstake, and weave up the sides. Finish off with your favorite rim.

If you want a longer, skinnier rectangle, just make more diamonds. The sample basket in the photo (previous page) has three diamonds, and illustration 39 shows four. Make however many diamonds necessary to attain the proportions you want for your rectangle.

You can vary the design by spacing the diamonds farther apart. Rather than connecting the center units, join the first row of diamonds surrounding them, as shown in illustration 40.

In illustration 41, the second row of surrounding diamonds connect. Diamonds can be designed into rectangular patterns however you wish.

Obviously, we're getting into variations already. There are many more in the "Diamond Variations" chapter. If you wish to do some further research on basic diamonds, look at some pattern weaving books (see the Bibliography).

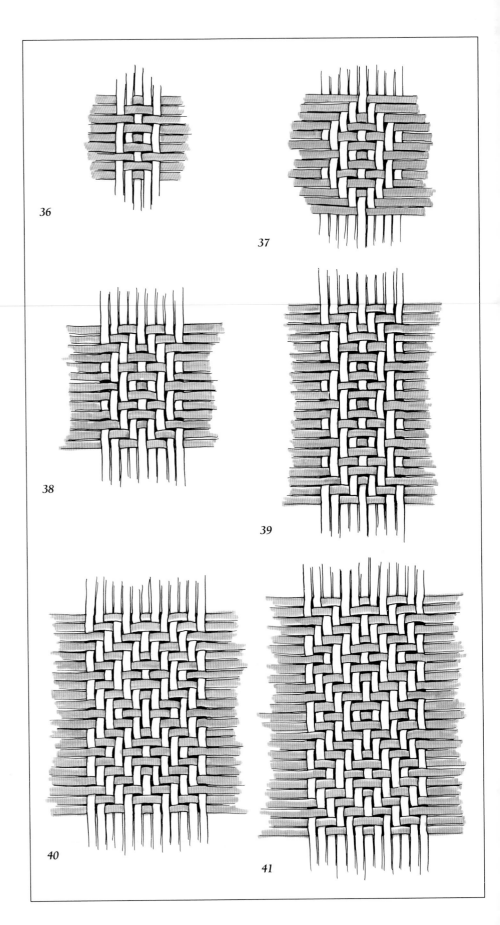

36

37

38

39

40

41

Basic Blocks

The center unit for a block twill is a set of four rotating "blocks." A block is a group of elements, each one shorter than the last. Together, the four blocks form a blunted diamond. Outside the

Anonymous, Tarahumara tribe from northern Mexico. Double-weave, 2/2 twill. Palm, 4" x 5" dia., old.

Basic Blocks

center unit, the weave becomes a regular twill, like an over two, under two twill.

Blocks are especially important because they can be bias plaited as well as straight plaited. This means they can also be woven into some interesting shapes. To whet your appetite, take a peek at the "Fun Shapes" chapter.

Blocks can vary in size from a 7-block all the way down to a 2-block. Which block you choose usually depends on your material. The width versus stiffness dictate how long a float you can tolerate. Until you develop a natural sense for floats, try to keep them down to one inch or shorter.

Measure your materials and estimate the number of elements just as you did for the diamond twills. Bias weaving is done on an angle, taking up more length, so add a third more length to be safe. Remember, too, that the base on a

Untitled sample by author. A 4-block twill. Flat reed, space dyed, 7" x 7" x 3-1/2", 1992. Photo: David LaPlantz.

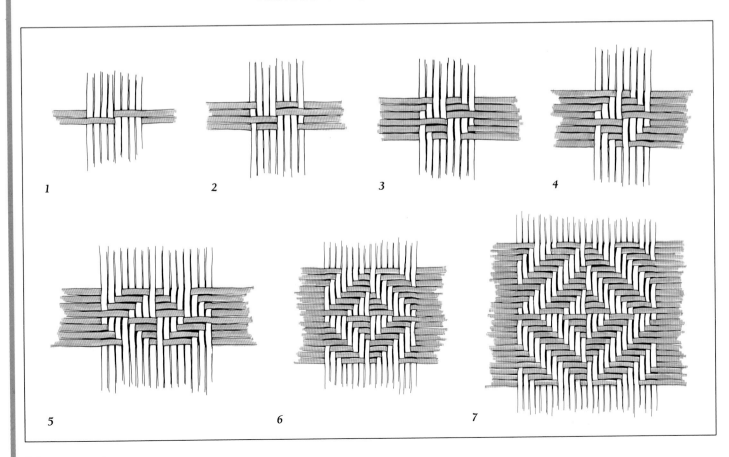

bias plaited basket loses one-quarter of its size, so plan on making big bases. Again, don't let a twill be your first plaited basket, either straight plaited or bias plaited.

4-BLOCK TWILL

A 4-block weaves over four, under four, and is referred to as a 4/4 twill. The block is a descending unit starting with four (i.e., over or under 4, then 3, then 2, then 1).

Increment: The increment is four, and there is no center element. Just add four elements to each side of the center, making 4 x 2 = 8 elements in each direction.

Start with eight elements. Since there are no center elements in block twills, weave on each side of the invisible center line. Using two new, separate elements, the first row is woven under four, over four. The other row is just the opposite: over four, then under four. Refer to illustration 1. As with the diamonds, you are weaving from the center of the base outward.

Add a row above and below the first two. To make a descending unit, these rows must weave over and under three. On the row above the two existing rows, weave over one, under three, over three, under one. Weave just the opposite below. Illustration 2 shows how the blocks start to descend.

To continue descending (illustration 3), weave over two, under two, over two, under two above the existing rows. Weave the exact opposite below.

To finish the descending unit (illustration 4), the next rows have to be "one's." They weave over three, under one, over one, under three above the existing rows, and the opposite below. Now that you've finished a unit, adjust the tension.

These last rows include "threes" at the edges. They're not complete yet; just ignore them for now.

Look at the weaving. Do you see the four blocks rotating around the center? This is your center unit; it sets up the stair-step diagonal for your twill.

Notice that there are pattern breaks both vertically and horizontally. These pattern breaks indicate the center lines of your basket, and they continue as straight lines throughout the basket. It is important to note, too, that the descending blocks are formed only at the pattern breaks; elsewhere the weave is a standard under four, over four.

Add four more elements on both sides, as shown in illustration 5. Continue to weave the elements in descending steps (4, 3, 2, 1) at the center line, or pattern break.

This time, add four more elements above and below. Maintain the twill pattern as you weave, and adjust the tension when you finish. (See illustration 6.)

Continue adding four elements to each side until the base is the desired size (illustration 7). Adjust the tension frequently, and use clothespins to hold everything in place.

When the base is finished, make sure it's exactly what you want before you weave up the sides.

Alternate Weaving Method

You can set up a warp and weave all the way across it, just as you did for diamonds. Set up a number of elements for your base that is divisible by eight (four for each side of the center line). Clamp or tape the elements to your work surface.

As shown in illustration 8, start in the center and weave under four, over four continuously until you reach the other edge. For the row below, weave just the opposite (over rather than under).

The next rows continue the over four, under four weave, but step in one element toward the center. For the top row, weave over one, under four, over four, under three, over three, under four, over four, under one. The row below is the exact opposite. Illustration 9 shows the pattern.

The next rows continue the pattern and step in one more element. The top row weaves over two, under four, over four, under two, over two, under four, over four, under two. Again, weave the opposite for the row below (see illustration 10).

The final rows (in this unit of fours) weaves over three, under four, over four, under one, over one, under four, over four, under three for the top row, and the opposite for the bottom row (illustration 11).

Continue adding elements until the base is the desired size. Remember to weave this loosely; then adjust the ten-

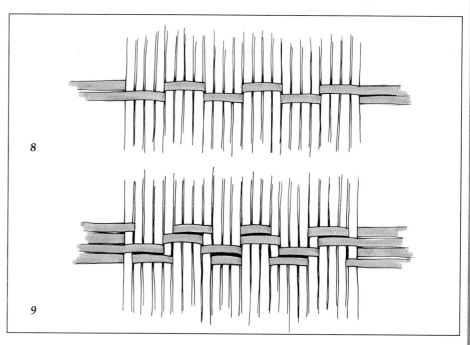

8

9

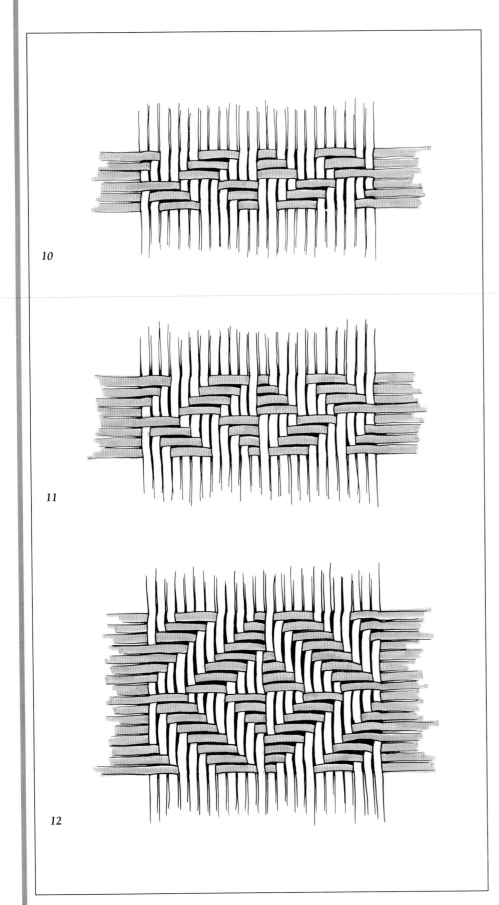

10

11

12

sion, starting in the center and working outward. Otherwise it can develop an uneven tension. Illustration 12 shows an even tension using this method.

Bias Plaited Sides

In bias plaiting, you divide each side of your base in half and weave the two halves across each other to make each side of the basket. In straight plaited twill, the sides show diagonal lines. In bias twill, the normally diagonal lines become horizontal ones.

TIP: You can ONLY turn bias corners at a pattern break. The weave won't work out right anywhere else in the pattern. This is an unexpected advantage. You don't have to count to find the halfway mark; it's at the pattern break.

Be sure to secure the corners of the base before you start turning up the sides. It's no fun if the base falls apart as you're trying to manipulate it. Clothespins or micro clips should hold everything.

Divide a side in half, as shown in illustration 13, and lay the two halves across each other. Be sure to look at the pattern, because you want to maintain it as you make the sides.

Start bias plaiting with the two center elements (see illustration 14). They already weave over four, under four. You want to continue that pattern. Whichever one is under four now weaves over four, etc. The one that weaves over four now weaves under four, etc.

Select the next two elements, one from each side. Look closely at their patterns. They're already starting to weave over or under, so let them continue. If the element is weaving over one, add in three more to make it weave over four. Do the same for elements that weave under. Illustration 15 helps make it clear.

Continue weaving the two halves across each other while maintaining the twill pattern. In other words, make all of the elements weave over or under four. Adjust the tension periodically and again when the side is complete.

Illustration 16 shows one side finished, and you can see how the twill pattern wraps around the side. Again, because

Untitled sample by author. A 4-block twill. Flat oval reed, 10" x 10" x 3", 1992. Photo: David LaPlantz.

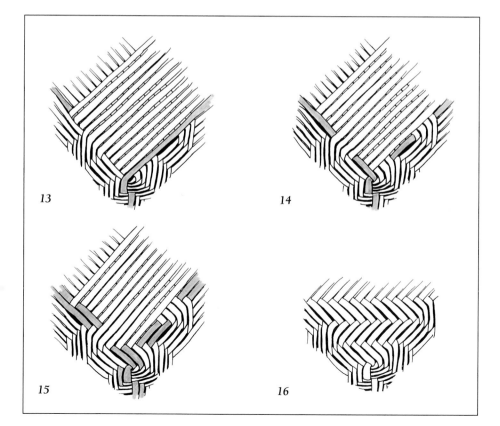

13

14

15

16

this is a twill, the lines in the bias plaiting become horizontal.

Repeat this process on all four sides. When they are complete, weave the overlapping ends together, still maintaining the twill pattern. Adjust the tension frequently. Weave all the way up to the top; then finish the basket with your favorite rim.

Straight Plaited Sides

Straight plaiting is the same for block twills as it is for diamonds. Weave a base and upstake; then weave a row around, overlap the elements, and clip off the excess. The only difference between blocks and diamonds is that blocks have pattern breaks in the center of each side, as well as on the corners.

Start by checking the base to see if the corners work out properly. If they don't, and if you want a firm corner, add one element to each of two opposite

17

18

19

20

*Untitled sample by author. A 3-block twill. Ash, 6" x 6" x 5", 1992.
Photo: David LaPlantz.*

sides, as shown in illustration 17.

Upstake (fold) all of the elements up firmly. With a new, separate element, weave a row around the basket (illustration 18). Be sure to maintain the twill pattern as you weave. Overlap the ends, and clip off any excess.

Using a new element, weave another row around the basket (illustration 19). Maintain the twill pattern, and adjust the tension. Again, I find it easier to control the tension if I weave the first three rows together, one side at a time, chasing style.

Be especially careful of the tension being generated. With floats going over four, there's a lot of room for movement. The elements can slip around, hide from you, and generally cause trouble. Keep them where you want them with clothespins or micro clips.

Weave up to the top, adjusting the tension frequently, and finish with your favorite rim. See illustration 20.

3-BLOCK TWILL

Three-block twills are essentially the same as 4-block twills. The basic weave is over three, under three, or 3/3. This time, the descending numbers start with three (3, 2, 1).

Increment: The increment is three for each side, making a total of six (3 x 2 = 6).

Starting with six elements, weave two elements across the center as shown in illustration 21. The weave is under three, over three for one row, and over three, under three for the other row.

Add a row above and below the first two. Maintaining the pattern, weave over one, under two, over two, under one for the top row and the opposite for the row below. (See illustration 22.)

Add two more rows, and maintain the pattern. As shown in illustration 23, weave the top row over two, under one, over one, under two. The opposite pattern is woven for the bottom row. Adjust the tension, and the center unit is complete.

Build outward from the center unit by

Untitled sample by author. A 3-block twill. Flat reed, 12" x 12" x 1-1/2", 1992.
Photo: David LaPlantz.

adding three rows to each of the four sides. Continue weaving the same pattern of over three and under three (illustration 24). As you weave, adjust the tension frequently.

Add groups of three elements to each side until the base is the desired size (illustration 25). Hold the elements in place with clips or clothespins; then choose either bias or straight plaiting. Weave up the sides, just as you did for the 4-block.

2-BLOCK TWILL

This time the basic weave pattern is over two, under two (2/2), and the descending numbers start with two (2, 1).

Increment: For the 2-block, the increment is two on each side, or 2 x 2 = 4.

Begin with four elements, and weave

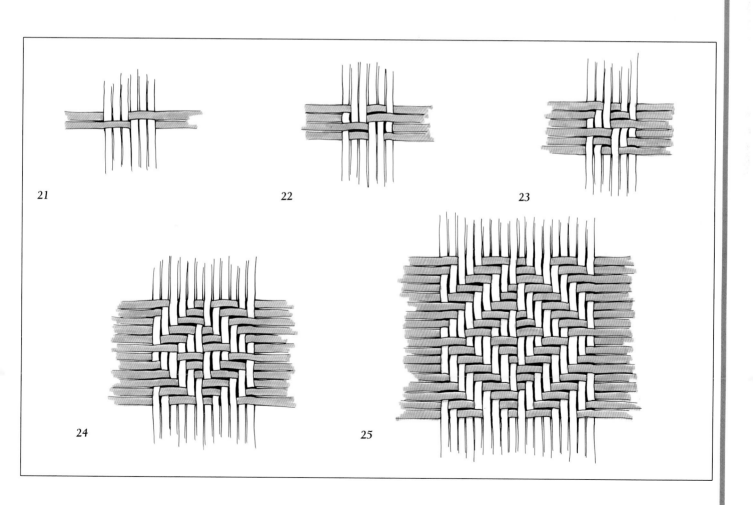

21

22

23

24

25

Above left: Untitled sample by author. A 2/2, 2-block twill. Microwood, 6" x 6" x 5", 1991. Photo: author.

Right: Untitled sample by author. A 2/2, 2-block twill. Microwood, 6-1/2" x 6-1/2" x 7", 1991. Photo: author.

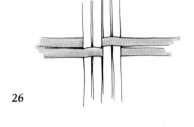

26

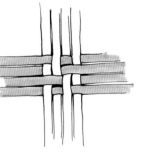

27

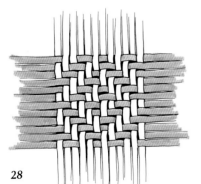

28

two elements across the center. As shown in illustration 26, weave under two, over two for the top row and the opposite for the bottom row.

Increase by another two rows. The top row weaves over one, under one, over one, under one. The bottom row is just the opposite. Illustration 27 shows the completed center unit. Adjust the tension.

Add groups of two elements to each side, enlarging until the base is the desired size (illustration 28). Always maintain the twill pattern, and adjust the tension periodically. Choose either bias or straight plaiting, and weave up the sides. Finish the basket with your favorite rim.

By now the progression should feel familiar. You can imagine a 5-block or a 6-block. When making block twills, you're only limited by the float length. The largest I've seen is a 7-block, but I've seen many of those.

VARIATION– RECTANGLE

To weave a straight plaited rectangle, you can simply stop early and make a rectangular, rather than a square base. It's a bit more complicated to weave a bias plaited rectangle.

Although it is possible to bias plait a standard rectangular base, the basket will not sit flat. Instead, it points down, creating a hanging basket or wall pouch.

To get a rectangular bias basket, you must start with a square base. Then don't divide the sides in half; divide them unevenly. Divide the sides as shown in illustrations 29 and 30, with the larger numbers adjacent to each other and the smaller numbers adjacent to themselves. (If you draw a line connecting the division marks on the illustrations, you'll see rectangles.)

Untitled sample by Sherry O'Connor. A 2/2, 2-block rectangle. Flat reed, 3" x 4-1/2" x 3-1/2", 1991. Photo: David LaPlantz.

Remember that bias corners can only be turned on pattern breaks. Consequently, we have to adjust the twill. To create off-center pattern breaks, the center becomes a series of "step downs."

The illustrations are for a 2-block rectangle, but any block size can become a rectangle. Just adjust your increments.

Increment: Here it is two, but the center unit can be any size. This is an over two, under two twill (2/2).

Start with the center "step down." Weave under one across a number of elements in descending steps. Illustration 31 shows four elements weaving across four elements. This creates a fat, almost square rectangle. To make a longer, thinner rectangle, step down (weave under one) across more elements.

Add two elements to each of the four sides. Illustration 32 shows how they form a 2-block above and below the center step down. (This is a variation on the 2-block twill.)

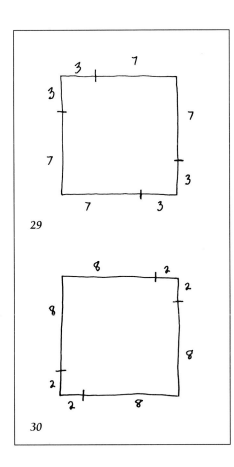

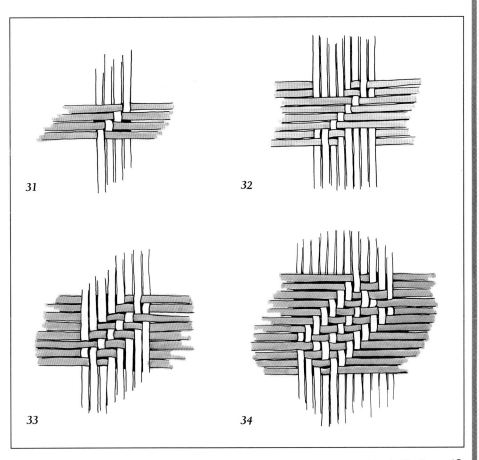

Untitled sample by Sherry O'Connor. A 2/2, 2-block rectangle. Gift wrapping paper and Sunday funny pages, 2-1/4" x 3-3/4" x 3-1/4", 1991. Photo: David LaPlantz.

Untitled sample by Sherry O'Connor. A 2/2, 2-block, with the base woven for a bias rectangle but the sides straight plaited. Flat reed, 5-1/4" x 5-1/4" x 4-1/2", 1991. Photo: David LaPlantz.

Now weave a row of twos (over and under) around the center step down unit (illustration 33). Adjust the tension.

Add two more elements to each of the four sides, and continue weaving the over two, under two twill (illustration 34). Make sure the tension is even.

Continue adding elements and weaving the 2-block twill until the base is the desired size. Illustration 35 shows the corners filled in for the base. Adjust the tension frequently, and secure the elements with clothespins or micro clips.

Bias Plaited Sides

Divide the sides AT EACH PATTERN BREAK (see illustration 36); then bias weave the basket. The twill pattern continues perfectly, just as it does with any bias twill basket. In addition, the basket will automatically become a rectangle; the pattern breaks dictate that. Finish the basket with your favorite rim.

Straight Plaited Sides

Despite its rectangular pattern, you have created a square base, and this can also be straight plaited into a basket. First, check the corners, and add two elements to two opposite sides, if needed (illustration 37); then upstake and weave. The off-center pattern breaks add a bit more visual movement to your basket, giving it a wonderful "extra."

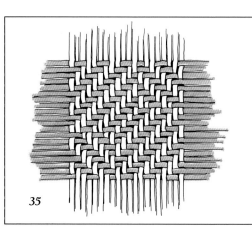

35

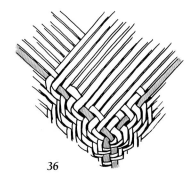

36

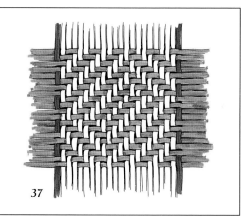

37

VARIATION— ONE-BLOCK

One-block? That sounds like plain weave. In this variation, the center unit is plain weave, or 1-block; the rest of the pattern is any basic twill. For these illustrations, an over two, under two twill is used.

It's easy to argue about whether this is a block twill or a "broken" diamond twill, but it doesn't matter what you call it. Since it has pattern breaks at the imaginary center lines and can be bias plaited, it's included here with the other blocks.

Increment: This variation has an increment of two and a center unit of two.

As shown in illustration 38, start with two elements weaving across two elements. Weave over one and under one—plain weave.

Next, add two elements to each of the four sides. Weave an over two, under two twill, remembering to descend to the 1-blocks at the pattern breaks (illustration 39). Adjust the tension, and weave in another round of two elements.

Continue to add elements, weaving the over two, under two twill until the base is the desired size (illustration 40). Adjust the tension, and secure the elements in place with clothespins or micro clips.

To make a bias plaited basket, divide the sides in half at the pattern break, and weave the two halves across each other. Maintain the twill pattern as you weave the sides together (see illustration 41). Finally, adjust the tension, and finish with your favorite rim.

Left: Untitled sample by Sherry O'Connor. A 2/2, 1-block (or broken-diamond) twill. Flat reed, 4-1/2" x 4-1/2" x 7-1/4", 1991. Photo: David LaPlantz.

Below: Untitled sample by Sherry O'Connor. A 2/1, 1-block (or broken-diamond) twill. Flat reed, 3" x 3" x 5-3/4", 1991. Photo: David LaPlantz.

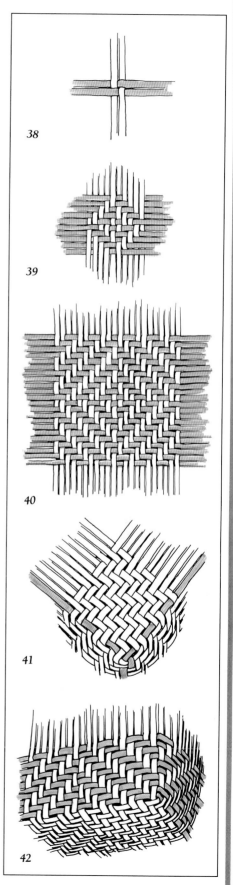

38

39

40

41

42

Untitled sample by Sherry O'Connor. A 2/1, 1-block (or broken-diamond) twill. Microwood lined with Mi Teintes paper, 3-3/4" x 3-3/4" x 3-1/2"--7", 1991. Photo: David LaPlantz.

Right: Untitled sample by Sherry O'Connor. A 2/2, 1-block (or broken-diamond) twill. Watercolor paper, 3" x 3" x 2"--7", 1991. Photo: David LaPlantz.

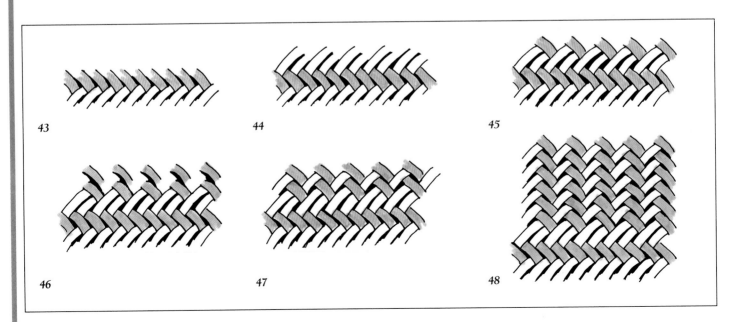

43

44

45

46

47

48

To straight plait the basket, upstake, weave a row around, overlap the ends and clip off the excess. Repeat for however many rows it takes to reach the top. A sampling of rows is shown in illustration 42. Adjust the tension, and finish the basket with your favorite rim.

VARIATION— VERTICAL VS. HORIZONTAL LINES

If we could only weave horizontal lines on bias baskets, the results would be boring, and our design capabilities would be very limited. Let's look at how to achieve vertical lines. The following instructions detail two different methods, but there are many others. Once you become comfortable with the overall technique, you can improvise your own method.

First Method

Find a straight line of "overs" in your weave. (Refer to illustration 43.) You can unweave or weave up to make a straight line. Next, take out any weaving above this line.

The next row becomes a series of groups consisting of two elements. In each group, one element weaves over two, and the next element weaves over three (see illustration 44).

"Cap" the groups by weaving over them; that means, weave over both elements of each group. Only every other element (in that direction) is used to cap the groups. The other elements are ignored for the moment. Refer to illustration 45.

As shown in illustration 46, the ignored elements now "step over one" and also weave over two.

Since you can't truly weave without elements in both directions, your basket looks like illustration 47 right now. However, you can see that you've already started the vertical lines.

Continue to step over one and weave over two, using every other element. (You can also think of it as weaving over two, under two.) Repeat the same weave pattern until the lines are as high as you wish (illustration 48).

Below left: Untitled sample by Sherry O'Connor. A 2/2, 1-block (or broken-diamond) twill. Braided bamboo, 4-1/4" x 4-1/4" x 6", 1991. Photo: David LaPlantz.

Right: Anonymous, Laos PDR. A 3/3, 4-block twill. Bamboo, 4" x 4" x 5", contemporary. Photo: David LaPlantz. From the collection of David and Shereen LaPlantz.

Second Method

This method also starts by finding a straight row of "overs" as shown in illustration 49.

Once more, work in groups of two elements. This time, the first element weaves over two, and the second weaves over three. See illustration 50.

Repeat this in the other direction. Again, working in groups of twos, weave over two and over three as shown in illustration 51.

Still working in groups of twos, the first element now weaves over one, and the second weaves over two (illustration 52).

Next, every other element weaves over two, capping off only the "over two" elements. Refer to illustration 53.

Now that the pattern to create vertical lines is established, you can add to the height of the sides using the same weave for each new row. (See illustration 54.) Step over one and weave over two with every other element. (You can also think of this as weaving over two, under two.)

Anonymous, Philippines. A 2/2 twill, no base. Straw, 8" x 12", collected in mid-1980's. Photo: David LaPlantz. From the collection of David and Shereen LaPlantz.

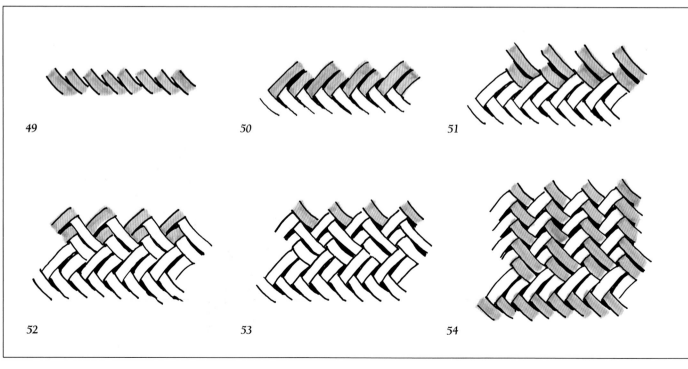

49

50

51

52

53

54

Folded Baskets

"Wave" by Keiko Takeda. Dyed flat rattan and ribbon, 14" x 14" x 6", 1989.

If you're not accustomed to twills and their tension, a good way to start is to weave flat pieces. Twills are easier to understand and easier to weave in just two dimensions. Make your first twills an enjoyable experience; make them easy.

To make baskets instead of flat mats, follow the bark bucket (or Japanese gift-box folding) traditions. Take a flat piece, and fold it into a basket!

You may wish to experiment by folding scrap paper before you actually work on your twills. My studio is decorated with hundreds of folded containers. You can develop some quick samples for yourself and keep them for a visual reference, a "pieces" dictionary.

Right: Untitled by author. Folding. Laminated rice paper, lace paper and abaca cloth, 9" x 7-1/2" x 4", 1990. Photo: David LaPlantz.

Below: Untitled samples by author. Folding with lacing and tying. Various papers, smallest: 4" x 4" x 2", largest: 9" x 9" x 4", 1989-1992. Photo: David LaPlantz.

Remember, bark buckets are sewn or laced together. A thin, flat element is lovely for sewing or lacing. The flatness of the element accentuates the technique.

FROM A SQUARE

Weave a square, in any twill pattern, and bind off the edges. Illustration 1 shows a square woven in block twill.

Fold the square into quarters in each direction. Next, fold and sew or lace the corners together as shown in illustrations 2 and 3: "a" to "a," "b" to "b," etc. If you choose something other than quarters for folding, your basket will be either deeper or shallower.

I think the basket is more interesting when the top is smaller than the base. To achieve this effect, fold the flat piece into quarters, just like you did above. This time, when you sew the corners together, grab in just a little beyond the fold line. See illustration 4.

To make this basket look different from the last one, I folded each corner point down (illustration 5). You need to work with a flexible material to manage the "down" gracefully.

To stay within the bark bucket tradition, the corners need to be sewn down flat. My favorite folded basket with flat corners tucks the tip of each corner *inside* the basket. The tips also need to be sewn down, which gives you a great design option. Each tip should be just about dead center inside a corner (see the "X" in illustration 6). What type of design do you want centered on each corner? Remember, embroidery and sewing techniques work as well as lashing methods.

I love pillow forms, and they are easy to make. Using a square, fold it into thirds in both directions. Referring to illustrations 7 and 8, fold "a" to "a." That's right, you're folding a side along itself. Lace the edges together. Fold "b" to "b" and lace together, etc.

What you have in your hands right now doesn't look like illustration 9 or the photo (next page), but it will. Put your finger inside the basket and open each corner

Untitled, flat sample by author. Various twills and satin weave.

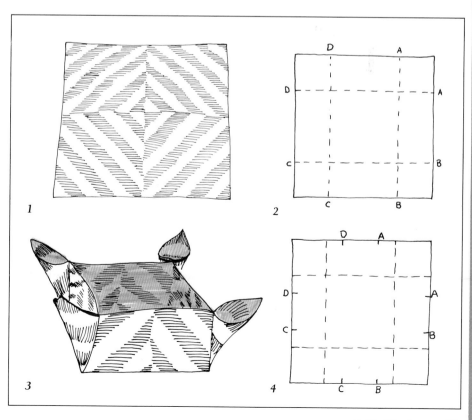

Author's flat sample (see photo on previous page) folded.

(they're probably folded together). Once the corners are opened, the basket should look essentially like mine. Wiggle it around a little more, adjusting the shape until it's exactly what you want.

FROM A PLUS MARK

Make a plus mark in any twill (see illustration 10). I tend to use "thirds" for the proportions, but sometimes the arms are a little shorter than one-third. Again, changing the proportions changes the depth of the basket. After you're finished weaving, bind off the edges.

A pillow basket develops when the arms are folded over each other and sewn down, as shown in illustrations 11 and 12. Consider using buttons as an embellishment when sewing one arm to another.

If the arms are folded up and laced

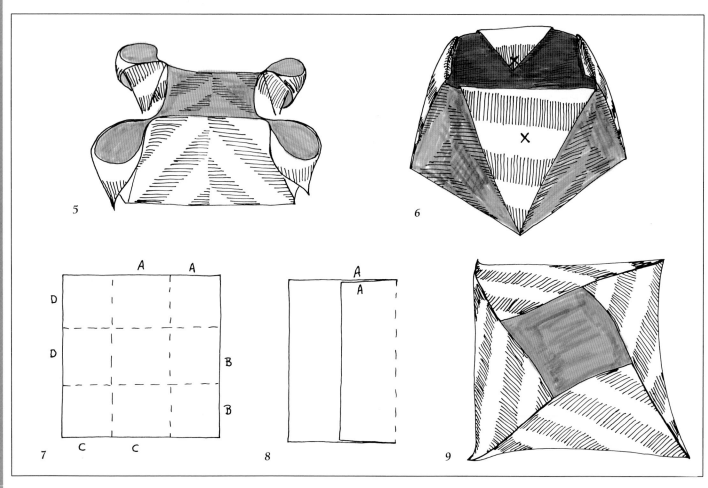

together (illustrations 13 and 14), a plain, simple box results. If you attach only the corners, then a small opening is left on each side. It's not as functional a basket, but it is interesting.

To show the difference in appearance if the top opening is smaller than the base, illustration 15 shows the same basket with the corners pinched in a bit. The sewing is away from the edge to emphasize the pinching.

The photograph on the following page shows a basket that is made from a plus mark with points (triangles) at the end of each arm. The sides are folded up, pinched together like a pleat, and whip stitched in place. The edges are covered to give it a finished look.

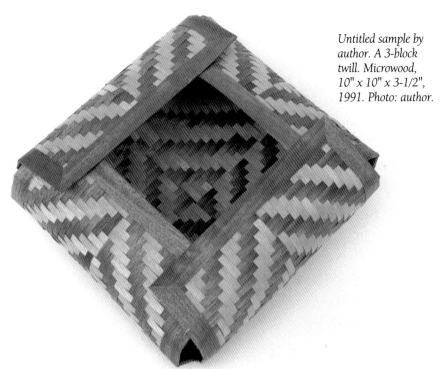

Untitled sample by author. A 3-block twill. Microwood, 10" x 10" x 3-1/2", 1991. Photo: author.

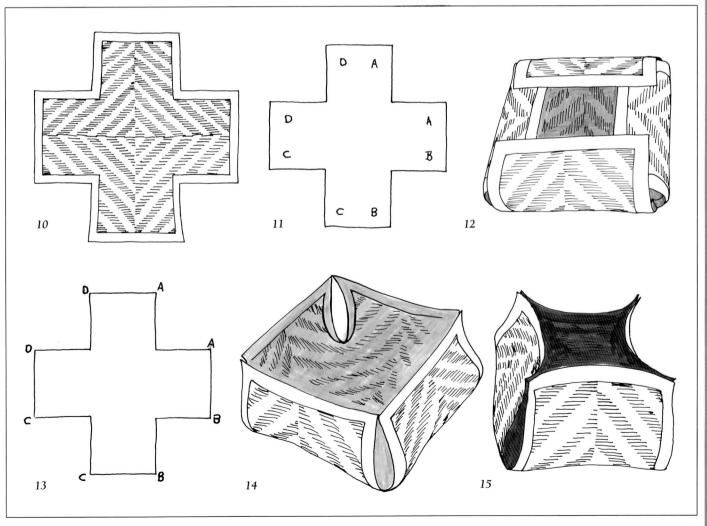

10

11

12

13

14

15

This winnowing tray from India, shown below, could have been folded as easily as woven. Think about what you want to make; it might be easier to fold rather than upstake and weave. Besides, if you make folded baskets, you'll be part of the bark bucket tradition.

Right: Untitled sample by author. A 3-block twill. Microwood, 6" x 6" x 4" (top spreads to 8-1/2" x 8-1/2"), 1991. Photo: author.

Below: Anonymous, winnowing tray from India, state of Orissa. A 2/2 twill. Bamboo, 12" x 20" x 2", collected in 1991. From the collection of Kathy Dannerbeck.

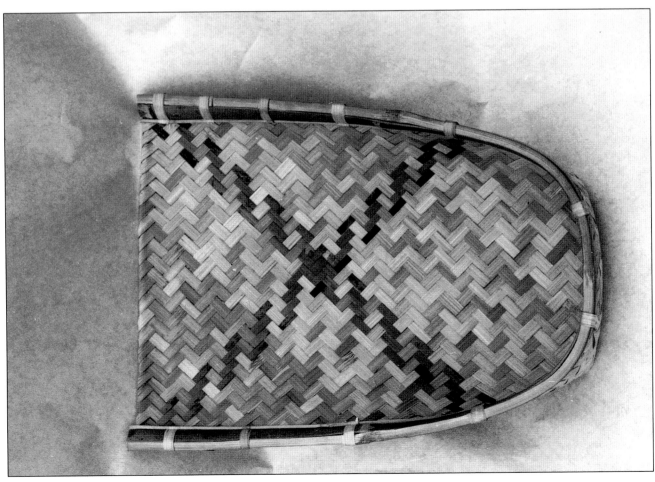

Obviously, people don't design twills or share twills with each other by carefully rendering the "overs" and "unders" as I have done for this book. There's a much quicker way.

Using graph paper, fill in the squares to match (indicate) your twill. It's easy to read when we look at the graph together with the illustration (see illustrations 1 through 4). To help you become familiar with reading them, graphed versions are included with many of the twills illustrated in succeeding chapters.

Graph paper filled in to indicate a twill (or any other pattern) is called a "pattern draft" or a "draft." This methodology comes from the hand-weaving tradition. In fact, there are a lot of weaving books focusing on patterns. Does this sound like a tip? They're great resources for ideas and techniques.

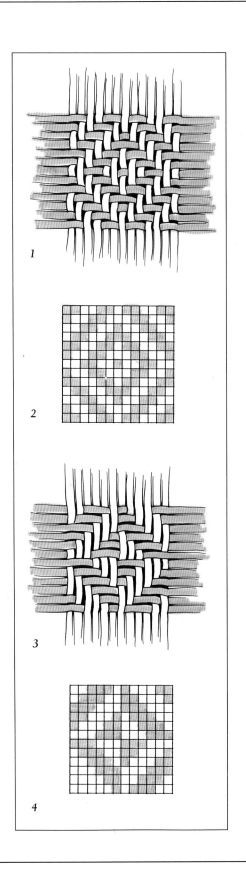

1

2

3

4

"Snakeskin" by David Blaisus and Jeanmarie Mako. Hand-pulled oak splints, uprights grayed with iron filings, 12" (incl. handle) x 11" dia., 1991. Photo: Rick Green.

Of course, there is a "right" way to read drafts (the dark areas should be the vertical "overs"), but I believe in options, rather than rules or limitations. When you make your own drafts, you can choose to make the dark areas in your drafts represent either the vertical or the horizontal elements. You must be consistent, though. If you choose to call the dark areas "verticals" then they must remain vertical for the entire basket. (Notice that I made mine horizontal—I like freedom of choice.)

When you start designing your own twills, you'll work frequently with the graph paper. I recommend using graph paper with squares that are large enough to see, like four or five squares to the inch. To save time filling in the squares, use a wide felt-tip pen. Those highlighting pens that are popular with college kids are great for drafting. Also, get plenty of liquid correction fluid. You'll make mistakes along the way, and whiting out an error is easier than re-drafting the whole pattern.

TIP: When following a draft, it's difficult to read across in a straight line. Many people use a ruler to help them read one line at a time. I fold my graph paper along the line I'm reading.

FLOATS

When you're drafting or developing a twill as you weave, floats will be your main limitation. There is no hard and fast rule about floats in basketry. As a weaver, I'm shocked by the length of some basket floats, but they work. The stiffer the material, the longer the float can be and still make a functional basket.

Early in my weaving career, I wove a very open piece for a costume design class. I planned to model it in a fashion show and was wearing it as I walked down the street to the event. Naturally, I got snagged—on some geraniums in a flower box! Now I always try to keep my floats short enough "not to get caught on any passing geraniums." I recommend you keep those geraniums in mind as you design twills.

The width of your material dictates your float length. For example, if you're using material that is one inch wide, and working an over two, under two twill, the float is two inches. If you change the width and use 1/4-inch strips (fettucini width), then the same twill will have a 1/2-inch float.

A 2-inch float is too long if the material is paper, but it's fine if you're working in hardwood splints or bamboo. A 1/2-inch float is fine for any material; in fact, it can be even longer.

The last variable is function. A basket that is used constantly, like a backpack, will be in snagging situations often and needs shorter floats. A purely decorative basket, one that sits on a mantle or inside a display case, can have dangerously long floats. Please beware; function can change. The basket we make to sit prettily on a counter may one day be taken out to the garden to collect produce.

In the beginning, I recommend erring toward shorter floats. As you get into the more complex twills, you'll be forced into longer and longer floats. If you've made a few simple twills with short floats first, then you'll be able to choose materials and widths that function with the longer floats.

Anonymous, men's beetle nut purse from Yap, Micronesia. Plaited twill with varied float length. Coconut frond, 18" x 18" (incl. fringe), 1978. Photo: Judy Mulford. From the collection of Judy Mulford.

Color Techniques

"Kaleidoscope" by Joan Moore. Rattan, 5" x 12" dia. (top), 1988.

Depending on how it is chosen, color can emphasize or it can obliterate the woven pattern. Color can also create new designs within the twill. Branching veins, shadowed boxes, and many more

1

2

3

"Zigzag Twill Basket" by Joyce Schaum. Rattan reed, 14" x 14" x 19", 1991. Photo: Gary Schaum.

images appear only through the use of color.

Sometimes you'll find drafting color patterns helpful. (You draft color patterns in full color.) Other times, you'll feel comfortable deciding on color as you weave. Some of the possibilities are illustrated in this chapter, but this is only a beginning. Experiment and explore; the possibilities are wide open.

THE BASICS

So far we've been working with one color in one direction and another color in the other direction. To see the effect of altering the colors, let's use a block that is an over four, under four twill (illustration 1), and a diamond and an "X" (explained in "Diamond Variations," page 90) that are

over two, under two twills (illustrations 2 and 3). The longer floats of the 4/4 allow more variation in colors.

COLOR VARIATIONS— CHANGING ONE DIRECTION ONLY

Illustrations 4, 5, and 6 show the colors alternating in one direction. Notice that the center two elements are the same color in the block twill. Because block twills are mirror images, the center elements (in both directions) must always be the same color. This is not true of diamonds or "X's," because they use a single center element.

Again, in illustrations 7, 8, and 9, one direction uses alternating colors, but in this

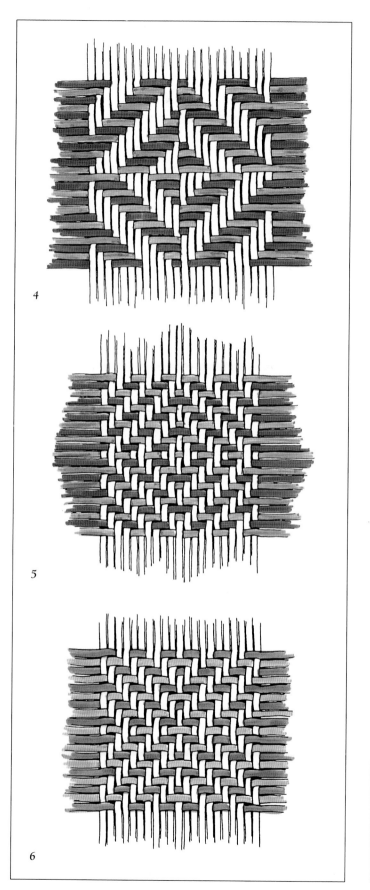

4

5

6

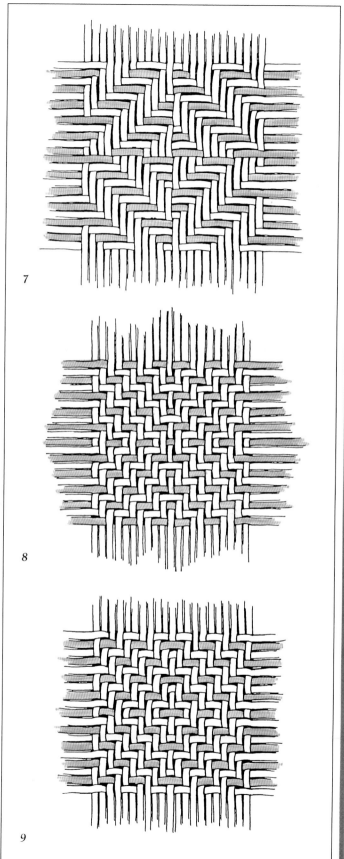

7

8

9

10

11

12

Untitled by Judith Olney. Reed, 5" x 14" dia., 1988. Photo: Roger Olney.

case, one alternating color is the same as that used for the other direction. If you have trouble seeing the patterns, try squinting when you look at the illustrations.

COLOR VARIATIONS— BRANCHING

In illustrations 10 through 12, alternating colors are used in both directions. With the diamond and the "X," the center elements alternate (vertical one color, horizontal the other). As noted earlier, all of the center elements in the block twill are the same color.

The colors don't have to alternate; illustration 13 shows them repeating every four rows. This is possible because the pattern is an over four, under four twill.

To demonstrate how important the numbers are, this 4-block repeats its alternate color every third row (illustration 14). It doesn't work for the 4-block, but it does, beautifully, for the 3-block (illustration 15). If you're having trouble with a color pattern, and you're sure it should work, check the numbers. A "three" repeat only looks good on blocks that are multiples of three.

With longer floats you can create fabulous color patterns. In a 4-block, four different colors can be used. In the example shown in illustration 16, the elements change from white to black downward, and from white to black upward. This type of color pattern can also work with a diamond or an "X," provided the floats are longer than two.

COLOR VARIATIONS— PLAIDS

Simple plaids can be made from two colors worked in groups. Compare the

Above left: "Wetumpka" by Billie Ruth Sudduth. Hand dyed flat and flat oval reed, 8-1/2" x 12-1/2" x 12-1/2", 1991. Photo: Melva Calder.

Right: Untitled by Tricia Brink. A 3/3 twill. Reed, 6-1/2" x 6-1/2" x 8", 1992. Photo: David LaPlantz.

13

14

15

16

17

18

19

"Zigzag Twill Plaid Basket" by Joyce Schaum. Rattan reed, 14" x 14" x 19", 1991. Photo: Gary Schaum.

results with the different weaves shown in illustrations 17, 18, and 19. The block appears more solid, and the diamond and the "X" have thin lines running through the colors. These variations are caused by differences in the float length.

Plaids can also use many different colors (see illustrations 20 through 22). For inspiration, look at plaid fabrics, skirts or afghans.

In the Chitimacha tray (opposite top), the design of the "X" pattern alters to highlight the plaid. While the solid color areas have large simple patterns, the two-color areas feature many small diamonds.

COLOR VARIATIONS— SHADOWS

Another example of a plaid tray (page 64) uses a lighter color to "shadow" the dark color, giving a three-dimensional effect.

20

21

22

Anonymous, tray, Chitimacha. River cane, 7" x 7" x 1", collected in 1982.

Anonymous, shallow bowl from Venezuela, Orinoco region. Unidentified plant fiber, 3" x 24" dia., collected in 1974. From the collection of Kathy Dannerbeck.

In illustration 23, the color pattern works against the diamond twill pattern to form boxes. The boxes in each quadrant are shadowed in a different direction.

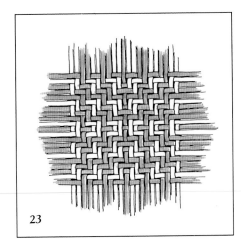

23

COLOR VARIATIONS—PAINTING

The patterns shown in these Indonesian baskets in the photographs are impossible. That is, they can't be done using elements that are all one color. To make these plaids, the elements are painted (in a pattern) so the colors will line up correctly. Space dyeing also works well.

To determine the painting pattern, draft the entire basket in color. Then measure and paint each element to fit the draft.

Painting can also be used just for highlights, and it can even be applied after the basket is finished. "Helter-Skelter" and "Fibonacci" (page 66) are good examples of this technique.

Left top: Anonymous, tray, Chitimacha. A 4/4 twill. River cane, 10" x 10", antique. Photo: author. From the collection of Nora Smids.

Bottom: Anonymous, nesting set of lidded baskets from Indonesia. A 2/2 twill with 7-blocks and diamonds. Bamboo, largest: 7-1/2" x 7-1/2" x 5", contemporary. Photo: David LaPlantz.

Anonymous, nesting set of lidded baskets from Indonesia. A 2/2 twill with some 7-block. Painted bamboo, largest: 7-1/2" x 7-1/2" x 5", contemporary.

Anonymous, lidded basket from Lom Bok, Indonesia. A 2/2 twill with "Lom Bok" written on lower right side of lid. Bamboo, 12" x 12" x 6-1/2", contemporary. Photo: David LaPlantz.

"Fibonacci" by Billie Ruth Sudduth. Hand-dyed flat oval and half round reed, 12" x 8-1/2" x 8-1/2", 1991. Photo: Melva Calder.

"Helter-Skelter" by Judith Olney. Reed and paint, 7" x 15" dia., 1991. Photo: Roger Olney.

"Wave" by Keiko Takeda. Dyed flat rattan and ribbon, 14" x 14" x 6", 1989.

"Basara I, II" by Keiko Takeda. Flat rattan and copper, I - 20" x 6" x 12", II - 15" x 6" x 16", 1992.

"Tunisia" by Christine Lamb. Plain weave interspersed with 3/3 and 2/2 twill. Rattan, 5-1/2" x 14-1/2" dia. at top, 1991. Photo: Charles Lamb.

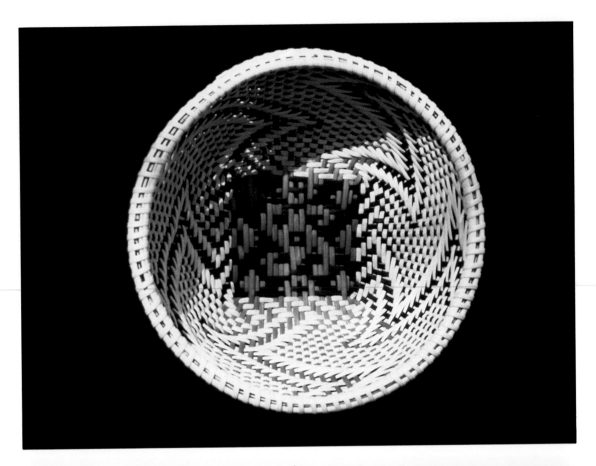

Anonymous, Philippines. Twill with overlay. Bamboo.

"Snakeskin" by Jeanmarie Mako and David Blaisus. Oak dyed with iron filings, 12" x 11" dia., 1991. Photo: Rick Green.

"Drury Lane" by Susi Nuss. Black ash and hickory, 12" x 12" dia., 1992.

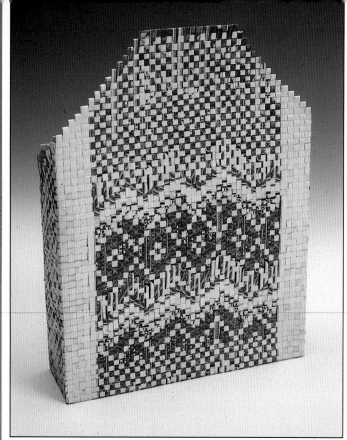

Opposite page, top left: "Diamond Back" by Zoe Morrow. Shredded money, 8" x 6" x 1-1/2", 1991.

Opposite top right: "Rippled Twill" by Zoe Morrow. Shredded money, 6-1/2" x 5" x 2", 1991.

Opposite bottom left: "Independence Twill" by Zoe Morrow. Shredded money, 5" x 2" x 7", 1989.

Opposite bottom right: "Zigging The Twill: To The Point" by Zoe Morrow. Shredded money, 6" x 2" x 6-1/2", 1989.

Left: "South Wind" by Betty Kemink. Reed, grapevine, and palm inflorescence, 24" x 35" x 6", 1991.

Below: "Sand & Surf" by Betty Kemink. Reed and honey-suckle, 29" x 18", 1991.

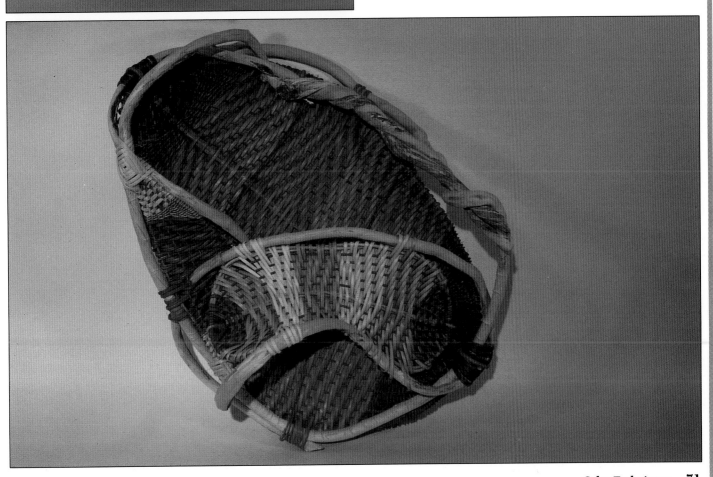

Left: "Reversal" by Lyn Siler. Reed, 10" x 10" dia., 1991.

Below: Untitled baskets by Judith Olney. Reed, L: 5-1/2" x 8" dia., R: 15" x 13" x 9", 1991. Photo: Roger Olney.

Above left: Anonymous, Philippines. Bamboo.

Above right: "Indian Patchwork" by Patti Hawkins. Reed, 5-1/2" x 10-1/2" x 7-1/2", 1992.

Right: "Snake on a Limb" by Lyn Siler. Reed, 6" x 12" x 10", 1992.

Far left: Anonymous, lidded lunch basket, Indonesia. Bamboo.

Left: Untitled by Jiro Yonezawa. Bamboo, cedar root, and cane, 8" x 4" dia. Photo: Toshihiko Shibata.

Below left: Anonymous, Cherokee. River cane, 6" x 6" x 8". From the collection of Lynn Stearns.

Below: "Tenju" (lifetime) by Jiro Yonezawa. Bamboo, cedar root, and cane, 7" x 7" dia. Photo: Toshihiko Shibata.

"Indian Quilt" by Joan Moore. Black ash, 2-3/4" x 2-3/4" x 2-1/2", 1989. Photo: Dick Moore.

"Star Quilt" by Joan Moore. Black ash, 3" x 6" dia., 1989. Photo: Dick Moore.

*Untitled by Joan Moore.
Reed, 12" x 12" x 3", 1991.
Photo: Dick Moore.*

*"Kaleidoscope" by Joan Moore. Twill
and undulating twill. Reed, 5" x 12"
dia., 1990. Photo: Dick Moore.*

Opposite page, top left: Anonymous, Orinoco region of Venezuela. Unidentified materials, 3" x 24" dia. From the collection of Kathy Dannerbeck.

Opposite top right: Anonymous, tray, Chitimacha. River cane, antique. From the collection of Nora Smids.

Opposite bottom: Anonymous, Tarahumara, Mexico. Double-woven twill. Pine needles and palm. From the collection of Kathy Dannerbeck.

Left: "Fibonacci" by Billie Ruth Sudduth. Flat oval and half round reed, 12" x 12" dia. Photo: Melva Calder.

Below left: Anonymous, Mexico. Palm, 10" x 11" dia. From the collection of David and Shereen LaPlantz.

Below right: "Playful" by Sosse Baker. Dyed and natural reed, 12" x 12" dia., 1991.

Right: "Sara" (I) by Keiko Takeda. Flat reed, 20" x 12" x 12", 1992.

Below: "Landscape with God's Eye Handle" by Sosse Baker. Continuous twill. Space dyed reed, 15" x 10" dia., 1991.

"Fake it" is the most important basketry technique I've ever learned. It's even more important in twills than in plain weave. Frequently, just when we're in the midst of a new variation, one that we love, the numbers turn out to be all wrong. (By the way, this can only happen if you start a new twill on the sides rather than develop one from the base.)

What can you do in a situation like that? You've woven all of the sides, except one last, little section that won't work. It's definitely time to "fake it."

Look carefully at these photographs of a basket from Guatemala, and you'll see what I mean. The first one shows the pattern as it is around most of the basket. The second one illustrates what happened at the end. When the numbers didn't work on the two main pattern rows, the artist created whole new designs.

On this lid, most of the pattern works vertically. Then, because the numbers didn't work out, the design "stretches" and becomes more horizontal.

Anonymous, Guatemala. A 2/2, 2-block twill. Palm, 9-1/2" x 8-1/2" dia., contemporary. Photos: David LaPlantz. Collected by Pam Niemi.

Anonymous, lid, Mexico. A 2/2, 4-block twill. Palm, 3" x 7-1/2" dia., contemporary. Photo: David LaPlantz. From the collection of David and Shereen LaPlantz.

Can you see the extra line up and down in this Mexican basket? I can't tell if the numbers worked out wrong, or if the basketmaker got mesmerized and changed patterns for a small section. This "fake it" is hard to see on the actual basket because of the colors; the black and white photograph really helps highlight the patterns.

Anonymous, Mexico, detail. A 2/2, 4-block twill. Palm, 10" x 9-1/2" dia., contemporary. Photo: David LaPlantz. From the collection of David and Shereen LaPlantz.

This pouch has the same pattern throughout, until you see the adjustment. All of these baskets came from the same area of Guatemala and Mexico. Because there are so many pattern "fixes," I'm suspicious that they've been done on purpose. In calligraphy, wonderful designs are used to cover errors (e.g., illuminated manuscripts). In the past, some calligraphers enjoyed the error-fixing designs so much, they made mistakes intentionally. These intentional flaws are called "conceits."

Perhaps a change in design would add movement and an interesting focal point to your basket. You don't need an error, or even a conceit, to use a different twill; you can design it into your basket. Meanwhile, when it's late in the day, you're trying a new variation and just discovered it won't work, don't go crazy. Fake it!

Anonymous, lidded case from Guatemala. A 2/2 twill, no base. Palm, 3-1/2" x 6-1/2" x 1/2", contemporary. Photos: David LaPlantz. Collected by Pam Niemi.

Diamond Variations

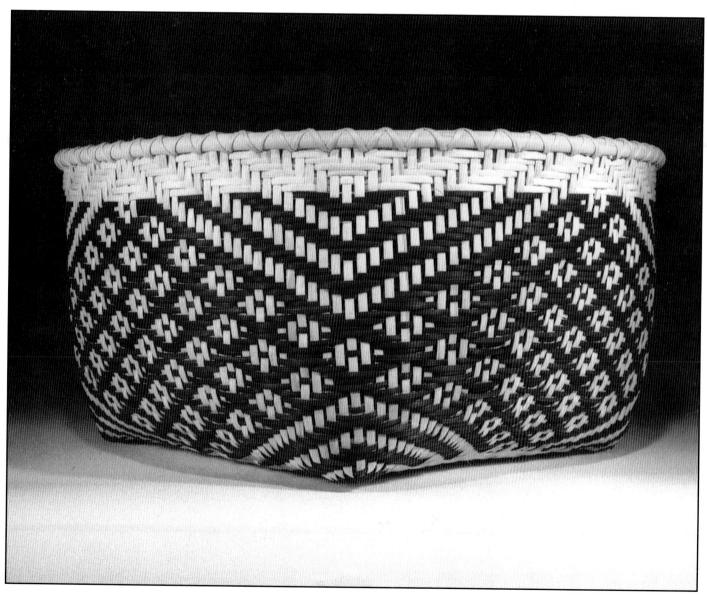

Untitled by Joyce Schaum. Reed, 22" x 22" x 12", 1991. Photo: Gary Schaum.

If you really were sitting here next to me, we would never have gotten this far without exploring more variations. Pattern variations are what make twills so interesting. In this chapter, you'll find some of the simpler ones. You may be able to weave them without a draft, or you may feel more comfortable making some draft-style notes.

These variations are not exhaustive. There are thousands of possible patterns, and this is just a sampling. If another variation occurs to you, try it.

BASIC DIAMOND IN THREE'S
(AND LARGER)

In the "Basic Diamonds" chapter, all of the twills were over two, under two. You can select a larger number and get a diamond with longer floats. Sometimes a diamond with longer floats looks stronger and more powerful. Diamonds can be worked in three's, four's, five's, and larger; just remember to consider the float length. Also, don't forget that the points have slightly longer floats (for the 2/2 twill the points are a three one pattern).

Increment: The increment for this example is three, with a center unit of seven. It is a 3/3 twill.

The center diamond looks and is woven essentially the same as the 2/2 diamond twill in the earlier chapter. Begin with the center unit—seven elements across seven elements. The center row is woven under three, over one, under three.

"Lidded Cherokee Patterned Basket" by Joyce Schaum. Rattan reed, 12" x 12" x 15", 1991. Photo: Gary Schaum.

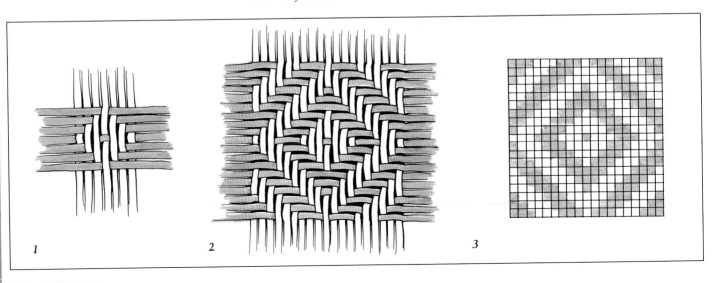

1   *2*   *3*

On each side of the center, weave a row over one, under five, over one. The next rows on each side weave over two, under three, over two. Finally, the outermost rows weave over three, under one, over three. See illustration 1.

Each point for a 3/3 diamond consists of three rows in a five, three, one pattern. From this example it is easy to visualize how to weave a larger diamond. Be careful of your float lengths, though. As the diamond grows larger, they lengthen correspondingly.

Continue with the 3/3 diamond by adding elements in groups of three to each of the four sides (illustrations 2 and 3). Maintain the over three, under three pattern throughout, and adjust the tension frequently. You can use this, and any variation, to create a base or a design element for the sides of your basket.

PLAIN WEAVE CENTER

Plain weave works effectively with twill, as a pattern variation, or to highlight a pattern area. Let's start by substituting plain weave for the diamond center. Obviously the diamond outline must remain (or the twill won't set up properly).

Increment: This variation has an increment of two and a center unit of nine. This is an over two, under two twill, but you can change that if you wish.

Weave nine elements across nine elements in plain weave—over one, under one. Be sure not to weave all the way out to all four edges; instead, create a diamond shape. (Refer to illustration 4.)

Add two elements to each of the four sides. Begin weaving the over two, under two twill outward from your plain weave diamond (see illustration 5). Remember to weave the three, one pattern at the points. Adjust the tension.

Add more elements to each side, and weave the 2/2 pattern until you reach the desired dimensions of your piece (illustrations 6 and 7). Be sure to adjust the tension frequently.

"Fiesta" by Christine Lamb. Plain weave interspersed with 3/3 and 2/2 twill. Rattan, 11-1/2" x 9-1/2" dia. (at top), 1990. Photo: Charles Lamb.

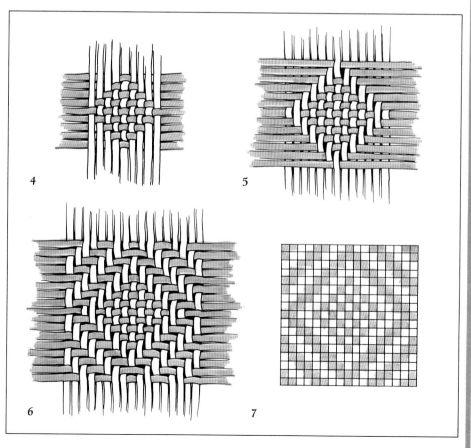

4

5

6

7

OUTLINING WITH PLAIN WEAVE

Christine Lamb's "Fiesta" (photo, previous page) uses plain weave to accent the diamond shape. Here the plain weave is so short, it almost hides. This emphasizes the twill.

Increment: The increment is three (two for the twill and one for the plain weave), with a center unit of five. This example is an over two, under two twill, but you can change that if you wish.

After weaving the center unit for a basic diamond, I like to weave another two rows around it (see illustration 8). It looks better that way, visually more

important, because it's bigger.

Add one element to each of the four sides. As shown in illustration 9, weave a row of plain weave—over one, under one—around the diamond.

Next add two elements to each side. Weave a row of over two, under two twill around the plain weave (illustration 10), and adjust the tension.

Continue to alternate the plain and twill weaving as shown in illustrations 11 and 12. Add single elements to weave a row of plain weave; then add two more elements, and weave a row of twill. Adjust the tension frequently as you weave. Repeat until you've reached the desired size.

MULTIPLE DIAMONDS IN THE CENTER

The center of your design can have more than one diamond. We've already made stripes of diamonds to create rectangular bases. Now let's try dovetailing (or crisscrossing) the diamonds. The illustrations outline each diamond with plain weave, while the basket in the photograph is outlined with twill.

Increment: It is two, with a center unit of thirteen across thirteen. An over two, under two twill is illustrated.

As shown in illustration 13, weave a basic diamond, five elements across five elements.

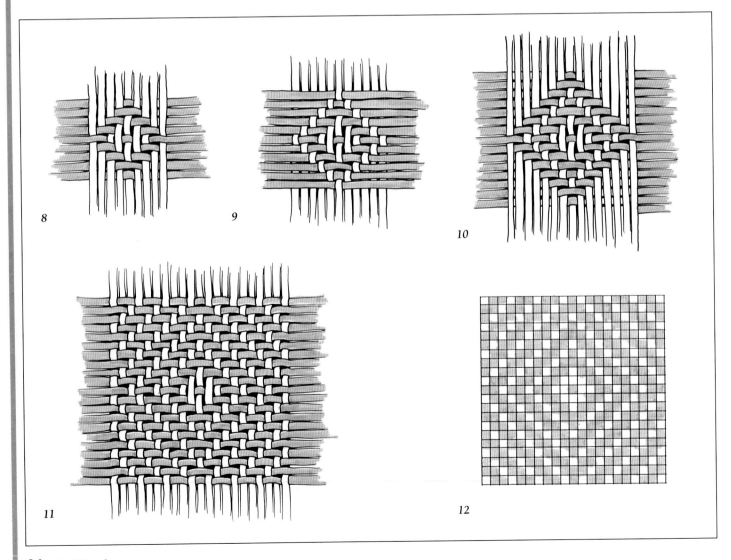

8

9

10

11

12

Add one element to each of the four sides, and weave a row of plain weave around the diamond. See illustration 14.

Add three more elements to the left side and to the bottom. Weave another diamond so that it shares one side with the first diamond. Outline the remaining three sides with plain weave. Refer to illustration 15. Notice how the side point of the first diamond becomes the top point of the second diamond.

Now add three elements to the other side. Weave a third diamond, placing it carefully so that it shares one side with the first diamond and a side point with the second. Again outline the new diamond with plain weave (see illustration 16).

Add three more elements to the bot-

Anonymous, Thailand. A 3/3 twill. Bamboo, 6" x 6" x 6", contemporary. Photo: David LaPlantz. From the collection of David and Shereen LaPlantz.

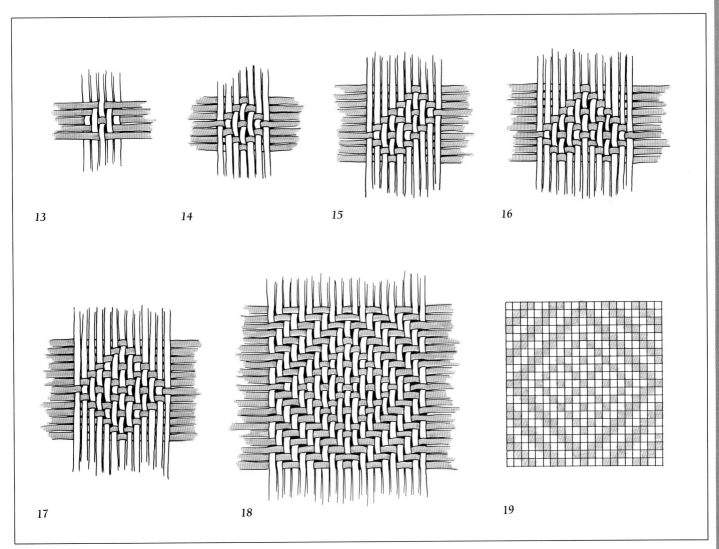

13

14

15

16

17

18

19

Anonymous, Indonesian place mats. Diamond and plus mark twills. Bamboo, 12" x 16", contemporary. Photo: David LaPlantz. From the collection of David and Shereen LaPlantz.

tom. Weave the final diamond, and outline it with plain weave. (See illustration 17.) You really only have to weave half of this diamond. The rest is already done! Adjust the tension.

Note: If desired, the center unit can include more diamonds. Just keep adding elements and weaving diamonds.

To finish the piece in simple twill, add elements in groups of two to each side. Weave an over two, under two twill until you reach the dimensions you want (illustrations 18 and 19). As you weave, frequently adjust the tension.

CONTINUOUS, DOVETAILING DIAMONDS

Obviously, if you can repeat the dovetailing diamonds as often as you wish for the center, then you can make a twill that consists exclusively of repeating diamonds.

Increment: For this variation, the increment is three (two for the diamond and one for the outline). There is no center element.

Weave the same pattern that you made for the center unit in the last twill, but don't stop. Just keep repeating the dia-

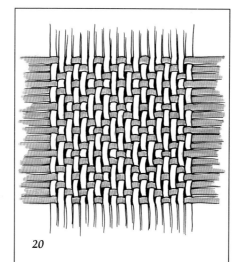

20

21

mond pattern until you attain the desired size. See illustrations 20 and 21.

MULTIPLE PLUS MARK DIAMONDS

Multiple plus mark diamonds work basically the same way that basic diamonds do. Be careful, though, the plus marks slip around when dovetailed. To prevent slippage problems, limit the number of plus marks used, or outline them with either plain weave or twill.

Increment: Here it is two, with a center unit of thirteen. An over two, under two twill is illustrated.

Working with three elements across three elements, weave a plus mark diamond as shown in illustration 22.

Add an element to each of the four sides, and outline the plus mark with plain weave (see illustration 23).

Continue to weave plus mark diamonds and outline them until the center unit is the desired size (illustration 24). You'll need to add three elements at a time to weave these diamonds.

With additional elements, weave an over two, under two twill around the center unit. Continue to the desired size, as shown in illustrations 25 and 26.

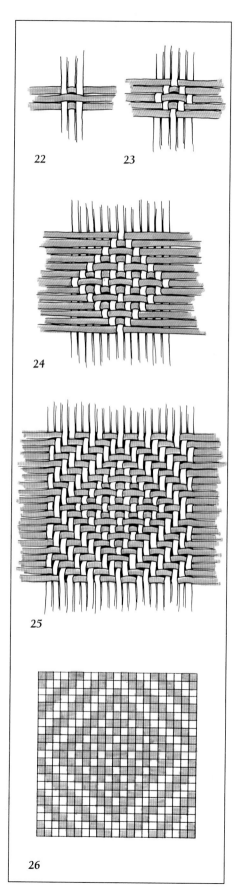

22   23

24

25

26

"Indian Patchwork" by Patti Hawkins. Reed, 5-3/4" x 10-1/4" x 7-1/2", 1992. Photo: David LaPlantz.

ALTERNATING DIAMONDS

The pattern in the oriental tray shown on the following page is slightly different than the dovetailing diamonds; there the colors reverse within the pattern. It may seem like a minor point, but this nuance can also be applied to other twills, creating a vast number of possible variations.

Increment: It's up to you; you can use this as a center unit and surround it, or you can repeat these diamonds for the whole pattern. An over two, under two twill is illustrated.

As shown in illustration 27, weave a basic diamond surrounded by a row of over two, under two twill.

Weave another diamond below it, connecting them at the point (see illustration 28).

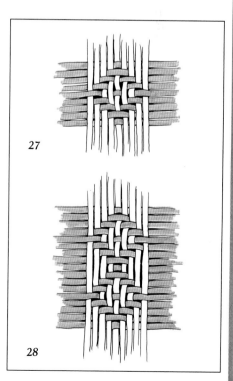

27

28

Anonymous, oriental tray.
A 2/2 twill. Bamboo, 1/2" x
15" (with handles), antique
store contemporary. Photo:
David LaPlantz.

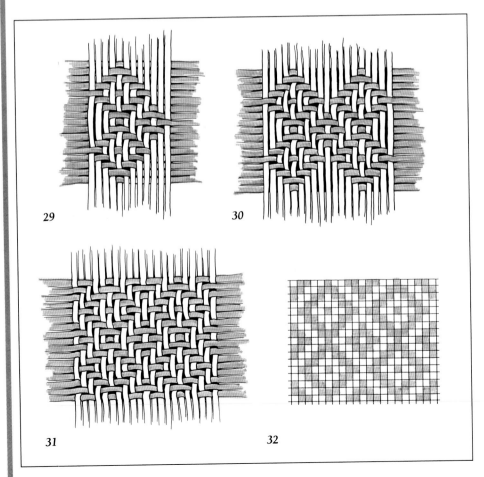

29

30

31

32

Weave a diamond adjacent to the first two (illustration 29). Do you see how it automatically reverses the colors (overs vs. unders)? Don't panic because the top and bottom points of the new diamond don't connect directly with the previous diamonds. They connect with the other (yet-to-be-woven) light diamonds.

Weave another two diamonds on the opposite side of the new diamond (illustration 30). Again the side points don't connect.

Continue until the center unit or pattern area is the desired size. Fill in the edges with partial diamonds, or surround the design with twill. See illustrations 31 and 32.

"X"—THE INTERSECTION

If four diamonds are put together, an "X" is formed where they intersect. That "X" can be woven as a twill.

Increment: The increment is one, with a center unit of three across five. Although this is an over two, under two twill, it can be built one element at a time.

Start with five elements. For the center row, weave under one, over three, under one. The rows above and below the center weave over two, under one, over two. Refer to illustration 34.

Add an element to each of the four sides. Continue the over two, under two twill, keeping in mind the three, one pattern required for the points (see illustration 35). You are, effectively, working four points at once.

Add another element to each side, and continue the twill (illustration 36). With these additions, the center polka dot shows up on each side. That sets up the next row of twill for the classic "X."

Continue the twill with another set of elements (illustration 37).

Add more elements and weave the 2/2 twill until you have the desired size. See illustrations 38 and 39.

"Star of Bethlehem" by Patti Hawkins. Flat oval reed, 8-1/2" x 8-1/2" x 14" (with handle).

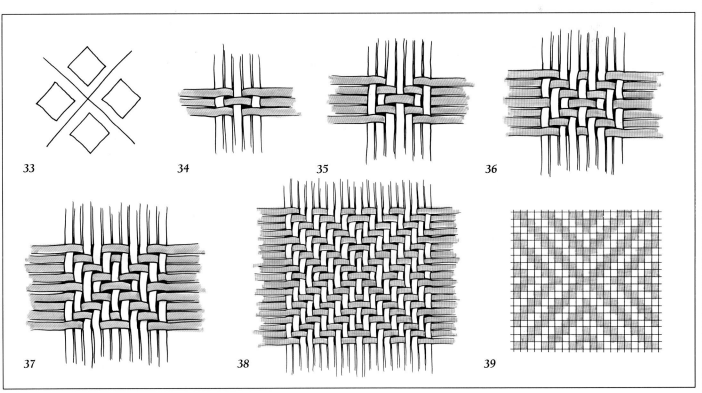

33

34

35

36

37

38

39

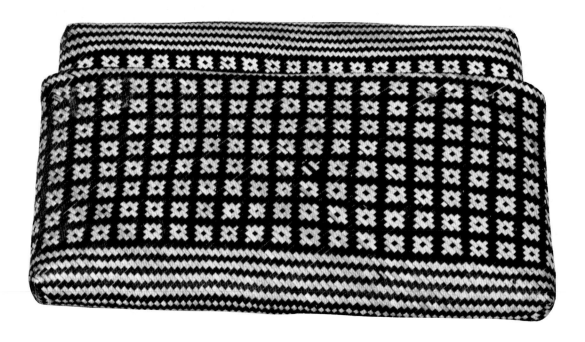

Block Variations

Anonymous, Belau purse, Micronesia. Sedge, 12-1/2" x 2-1/2" x 7", 1991. Photo: Judy Mulford. From the collection of Judy Mulford.

Block twills worked with plain weave and dovetailing blocks are among the most beautiful twill variations. If you wish to pursue this style of twill further, look at baskets done by natives of the South

Pacific Islands or the Maori of New Zealand. Their work in block twills is stunning.

PLAIN WEAVE OUTLINE

Block twills are just as easy to surround with plain weave as are diamonds, but the results are quite different.

Increment: The increment is four (three for the twill and one for the plain weave), with a center unit of six. This is a 3-block twill—over three, under three.

As shown in illustration 1, weave six elements across six elements, making a basic 3-block center.

Add one element to each of the four sides, and put in a row of plain weave around the blocks. (See illustration 2.)

Continue by adding three elements to each side. Weave an over three, under three twill. Now add another element, and make a row of plain weave. Repeat, alternating twill and plain weave, until you reach the desired size. (See illustrations 3 and 4.) As the woven area grows, notice what happens to the colors. Each quadrant takes on a dominant color.

ONE-BLOCK WITH PLAIN WEAVE OUTLINE

This is essentially the same as the above pattern, but with a 1-block (or broken-diamond) twill. Any size block twill can be outlined with plain weave.

Increment: Here it is three (two for the twill and one for the plain weave), with a center unit of two. This is an over two, under two twill.

Using two elements in each direction, weave over one, under one for the center unit. Add two elements to each of the four sides, and weave a row over two, under two. Using another four elements, one added to each side, surround the twill with a row of plain weave. Refer to illustration 5.

Continue to alternate twill and plain

Untitled sample by Sherry O'Connor. A 2/1, 1-block (or broken-diamond) twill. Flat reed, 7" x 7" x 2-1/4", 1991. Photo: David LaPlantz.

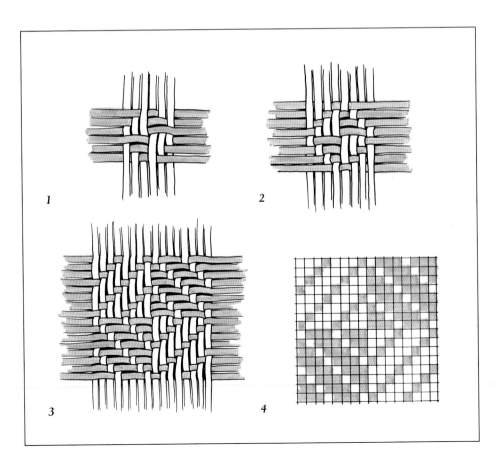

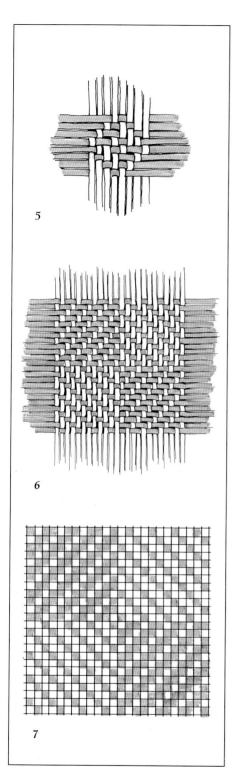

5

6

7

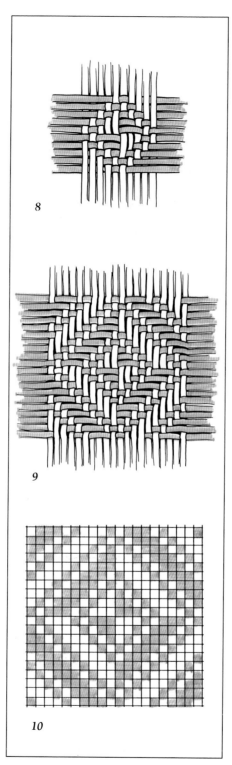

8

9

10

one will work with this type of twill.

Increment: For this example, the increment is five (three for the twill and two for the plain weave), with a center unit of six. If you want more rows of plain weave, increase the increment accordingly. This is a 3-block, over three, under three twill.

After you weave a 3-block center unit, add two elements to each of the four sides. This time, make two rows of plain weave around the center blocks. See illustration 8.

Continue to weave a row of over three, under three twill and surround it with two rows of plain weave (illustrations 9 and 10). Add elements in increments of five, and adjust the tension periodically.

PLAIN WEAVE WITH BLOCK-ON-BLOCK (DOVETAILING BLOCKS)

When blocks dovetail, the pattern is called block-on-block. Numbers are critical for this type of twill because if the numbers aren't right, you'll get partial blocks. For a 3-block twill, it works to have two rows of plain weave surrounding the blocks. (There's an example of this twill in the "Fun Shapes" chapter; it's the juxtaposed squares basket.)

Increment: The increment is six (four for the block-on-block twill and two for plain weave), and the center unit is six. A 3-block is illustrated.

As shown in illustration 11, weave a basic 3-block center, and surround it with a row of plain weave.

With a new element added to each side, make a second row of plain weave around everything. Add another element to each side, bringing the total to twelve in each direction. Now weave the edges into blocks (two 3-blocks per side). Refer to illustration 12. Notice how simple it is; just pick up the corner three elements, and weave them over or under the others.

As shown in illustration 13, add three more elements to each side, and weave another set of blocks (three 3-blocks per side). These form a stair-step diagonal for the outer edge. You've now built a block on a block.

weave as shown in illustrations 6 and 7. Add two elements and weave a row of twill; then add another element and weave a plain row. Once again, there is still a dominant color for each quadrant. That happens whenever a single row of plain weave is used for outlining.

MORE OUTLINING IN PLAIN WEAVE

If you like the plain weave outline but don't want the quadrants dominated by a single color, use two or more rows of plain weave. Any number of rows greater than

Anonymous, Philippine floor mat. Block twills. Lauhala, 23" x 23", collected mid-1980's. Photo: David LaPlantz. From the collection of David and Shereen LaPlantz.

This pattern continues to grow by adding the increment of six in three distinct steps. First, add two elements to each side, and make two rows of plain weave. Then add one element, and make blocks out of the "fringe." Finally, add three elements, and weave a second row of blocks. Refer to illustrations 14 and 15 to see the total pattern.

WIDER PLAIN WEAVE WITH BLOCK-ON-BLOCK

You can use more than two rows of plain weave between the blocks, but, again, the numbers are critical. For a 3-block twill, you must start with two rows of plain weave, then increase by increments of three. That means, you can use 2 + 3 = 5 rows (or 8, 11, 14, etc.).

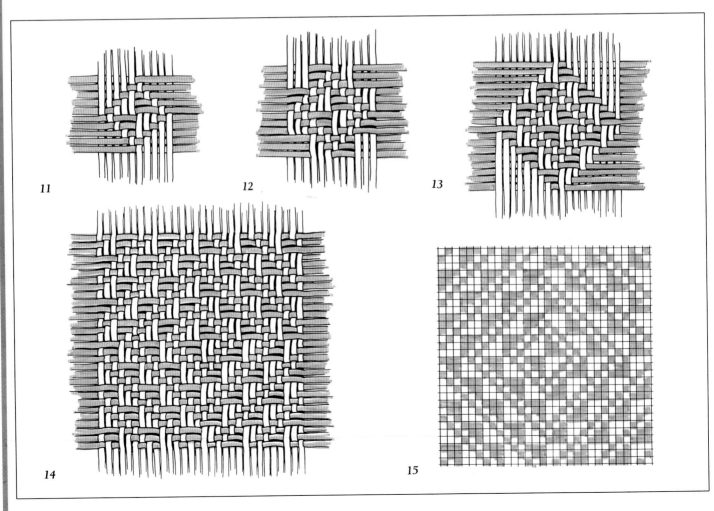

11

12

13

14

15

Increment: Make your own choice for the increment.

Wider bands of plain weave are created using the same techniques described for the last pattern. When you get to the plain weave rows, simply add more elements and weave more rows. (See illustrations 16 and 17.)

The pattern of this Maori purse (photograph at right) is somewhat hard to see because of its dark, blue-green color. The pattern is a block-on-block separated with a single row of plain weave. Since the pattern is confined to an area instead of running continuously throughout, the numbers aren't important. Nothing has to match up.

Anonymous, Maori purse from New Zealand. Plain weave with 5-block twill. New Zealand flax, 12" x 5" x 1/2", contemporary. Photo: author.

16

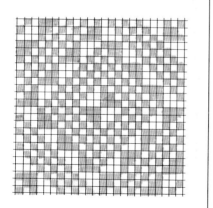

17

CONTINUOUS BLOCK-ON-BLOCK

The block-on-block (or dovetailing) pattern can be an overall design as well as a border. An overall design keeps repeating until the entire surface is covered. (There's an example of this twill in the "Folded Baskets" chapter.)

Increment: This increment is more complex than others so far. It is three on each side, and one plus three on top and bottom. A 3-block twill is illustrated. You can use another size block if you choose, but the increment changes accordingly.

Start by weaving the basic 3-block center as shown in illustration 18.

Add one element to the top and one to the bottom. Maintain the weave (i.e., if the other "leftover" elements are overs, let the new element be an over, etc). Notice how the ends automatically make this into a set of blocks. See illustration 19.

Now add three elements to each side, and weave them in as alternating blocks. Check illustration 20 for the pattern.

There really is no other way these blocks can weave and still be opposite each other. The longest floats, in any direction, are three. If any float is longer, it's signaling an error.

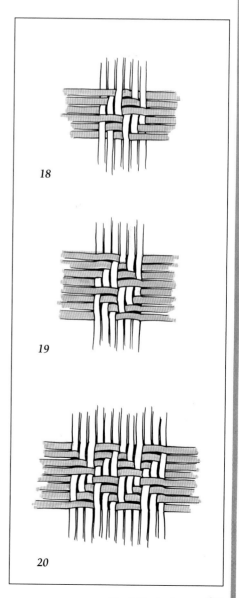

18

19

20

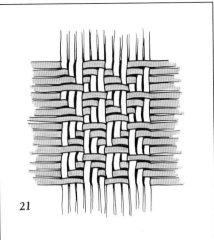

21

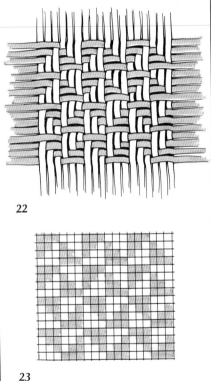

22

23

turned on each and every pattern break, this twill has many possibilities.

COMBINING BLOCK SIZES

Blocks can be combined almost any way you choose. You can even build outward by increasing the block's size. Start with a 2-block, surround it with 3-blocks, and finish with 4-block corners. (There's an example of this pattern in the "Words of Caution" chapter.)

Increment: It varies and grows.

As shown in illustration 24, start by weaving a 2-block center.

Next add one element to each side as shown in illustration 25. By maintaining the weave, the new elements automatically form 3-blocks, just as they do for the block-on-block twill.

Increase by four elements on each side. In the center of each side, weave a unit of four dovetailing blocks using 3-block twill. See illustration 26.

Each corner becomes two more blocks (illustrations 27 and 28). The inner one is a 3-block, and the "corner-most" is a 4-block. This is where the pattern must stop. Although it seems like this progression could continue, the numbers just don't work.

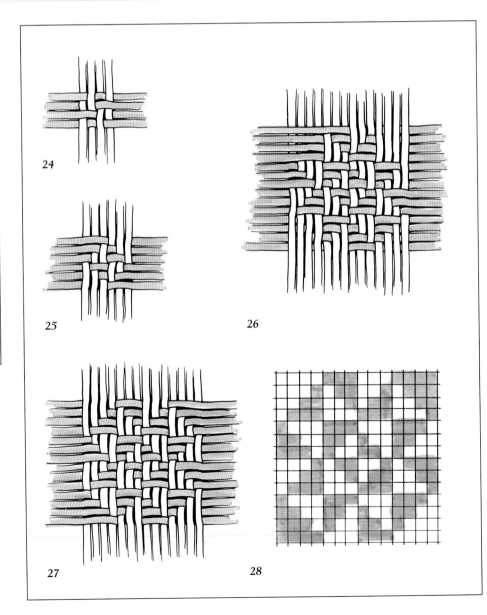

24

25

26

27

28

Next, weave four elements as alternating blocks on the top and bottom (illustration 21).

Continue adding three elements to the sides and weaving alternating blocks. Then add four elements to the top and bottom, and weave alternating blocks (see illustrations 22 and 23). Because it employs two different increments, this pattern results in a rectangle.

This pattern is particularly good for making exotic shapes because of all the pattern breaks. Since bias corners can be

Building Complex Twills

At this point, you know enough twill patterns to combine them, building more complex twills. It's not difficult; in fact, many beautiful combinations can be made without even drafting. Just weave a center and surround it with another twill. Add new patterns as the basket grows.

Before we get into building complex patterns, let's look at some of the design options. There are three ways to think about using pattern on a basket (also called coverage methods): (1) as a spot of pattern, (2) as a continuous stripe of pattern, or (3) as an overall pattern.

A spot of pattern or a pattern area is surrounded by plain weave or plain twill. Because they are visually stronger than what surrounds them, pattern areas become highlights. Where they're placed becomes an important design decision.

A continuous stripe of pattern is a border. When on the sides, these stripes run around the entire basket. When used on the base, they surround the center unit or a larger design. Using a series of borders is the easiest way to build a complex twill. Use one twill for the first stripe, another twill for the next stripe, and a third for the following. Stripes tend to work best visually if the largest or heaviest-looking one is on the bottom, and the smallest is near the rim.

An overall pattern is a repeating design that may or may not be a dovetailing design. For example, basic twills use diagonals as an overall pattern, while block-on-block twills use a dovetailing block. An overall pattern covers the entire basket, both base and sides.

When designing your own twills, first decide which method of coverage to use; then design the twill.

These Guatemalan bottles illustrate how easy it is to build a twill through continuous pattern stripes. The more complex bottle uses a wider, darker stripe near the bottom to add visual weight to the

Far left: Anonymous, covered bottle, Guatemala. A 2/2 twill. Palm, 11-1/2" x 3" dia., contemporary. Photo: David LaPlantz. Collected by Pam Niemi.

Left: Anonymous, covered bottle, Guatemala. A 2/2 twill. Palm, 10" x 2-1/2" dia., contemporary. Photo: David LaPlantz. Collected by Pam Niemi.

base. Smaller stripes near the top make that area feel lighter. A wider stripe at the neck's base visually helps the neck to sit on the bottle.

Notice how many different twills are used. In addition, some twills are dark for one stripe and light for another, giving them a totally different appearance. There's no limit to how many different twills you can use on the sides of your basket.

One more design tip—on the simpler basket, notice how the pattern units don't stack up directly on top of each other. This gives the basket much more "movement." Think of the same pattern with everything straight and perfectly aligned; it would look static and much less interesting.

The tray shows both a grouping of separate patterns in the center unit and a continuous stripe. Although it's used here to make a tray, this complex twill pattern could also be used for the side of a basket. If you use a pattern area on the side, consider surrounding it with a con-

Anonymous, tray, China. Various twills. Bamboo, 1-1/2" x 15" dia., contemporary. Photo: David LaPlantz. From the collection of David and Shereen LaPlantz.

tinuous stripe. Bordering something, even a basic twill, highlights it, telling the viewer that this is an important area to notice.

This folder from the Philippines has pattern areas surrounded by plain weave. One pattern area is almost a stripe, and there is a continuous stripe near the base. Visual interest is heightened through the use of color. A dark-colored, thin element is slipped in as an overlay to highlight the pattern.

Color is used more dramatically in this floor mat. Here the designs are spots, rather than continuous stripes. The amount of pattern also varies; the short stripes have short patterns, and the long stripes have longer patterns. That gives a lot of movement to this piece.

After looking at several examples, it is obvious that complex twills are the natural result of an interest in, and comfort with, twill's many variations. In many cases, the intricate-looking designs are merely the result of combining several twill patterns in one basket.

SPREADING YOUR TWILL TO THE EDGES

Let's take a quick look at what to do with a pattern you've developed. The pattern will probably be in a diamond shape, and that's not the shape of your base or the sides of your basket.

First develop a pattern. An example is given in illustration 1. You will find that it is easier to use a draft to create your design. That way you can make sure the numbers work before starting to weave.

The design you develop can become a spot of pattern by simply weaving any basic twill (diagonal lines) to the outer edges. See illustration 2.

Alternatively, the pattern can be repeated out to the edges as shown in illustration 3. When the pattern wraps around the edges and corners, it creates a smaller version of the center, as a triangle, on each corner.

There's no reason to stop developing a pattern just because you've reached the edge. Keep adding new borders (illustration 4 shows several). They won't appear entirely on the base; instead, they'll complete themselves on the sides. If you add so many that they won't complete themselves on the sides, that's fine too.

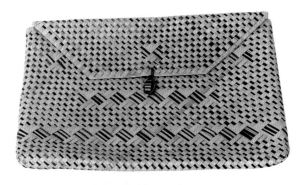

Left top: Anonymous, Philippine folder. Plain weave with twill accents. Lauhala and bacbac, 10" x 15" x 1/2", collected mid 1980's. Photo: David LaPlantz. From the collection of David and Shereen LaPlantz.

Bottom: Anonymous, floor mat, Philippines. Plain weave with twill areas. Lauhala, 22" x 34", contemporary. Photo: David LaPlantz. From the collection of David and Shereen LaPlantz.

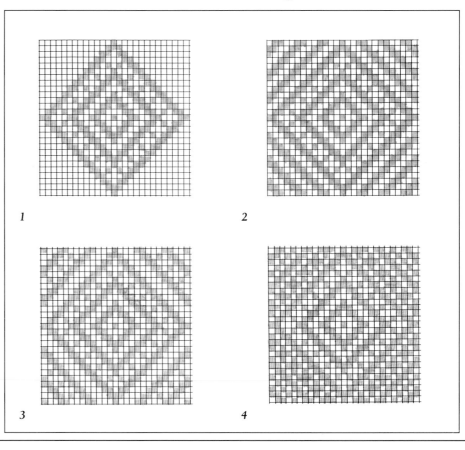

1

2

3

4

Lines, Lines, Lines

Twills have a linear quality. So far we've only used lines to form diamonds, but there are other options. You can use twill to make lines spiral or zigzag around your basket.

"Lightning" by Sosse Baker. A 1/1/1/4 continuous twill. Dyed and natural flat oval reed, 22" x 22" x 22", 1991. Photo: Sosse Baker.

Lines, Lines, Lines

The easiest way to spiral lines around your basket is to start the pattern on the sides—don't try to bring it up from the base. Weave any basic base; then change the pattern when you upstake. Twills naturally form diagonal lines, and if the twill lines only go in one direction, they automatically spiral around the basket.

You have to be very careful of the numbers; each side must be divisible by the increment you've chosen. How do you know your increment? Each pattern has "overs" and "unders." Add them together to get your increment.

That means, if you're developing a linear twill of over three and under one, the increment is four. If your pattern is over two, under one, over one, under two, the increment is six.

I recommend checking your math and counting the elements a couple of times. Hopefully this never happens to you, but when I get all involved in weaving, I can make some amazing math errors.

THE LINEAR TWILL BASE

Setting up a base for a linear twill to wrap up the sides is just a little bit different from anything we've done so far. Unlike other twills, linear designs don't just start in the center and weave outward.

"Tsubo" by Keiko Takeda. Dyed flat rattan and arrowroot, 14" x 14" x 30", 1990.

Untitled sample by author. A 3/1 twill. Microwood, 4-1/2" x 4-1/2" x 4-1/2", 1992. Photo: David LaPlantz.

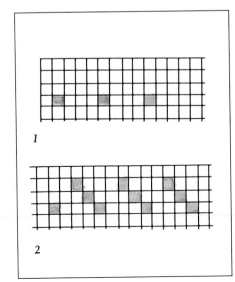

1

2

I recommend drafting your pattern first, before weaving it.

Begin by determining the twill pattern you want to have on the sides. The sample basket in the photograph (left) and the first illustration both show an over three, under one (unbalanced) twill.

Next decide which direction the twill should take. As shown in illustration 2, I like to draft about three rows to establish the direction.

Now let's look at the structure of a basket (illustrations 3, 4, and 5). If the basket has a square base and straight sides, it looks like a box. When the sides are flattened out, the overall shape becomes a plus mark. Therefore, when you're drafting the sides,

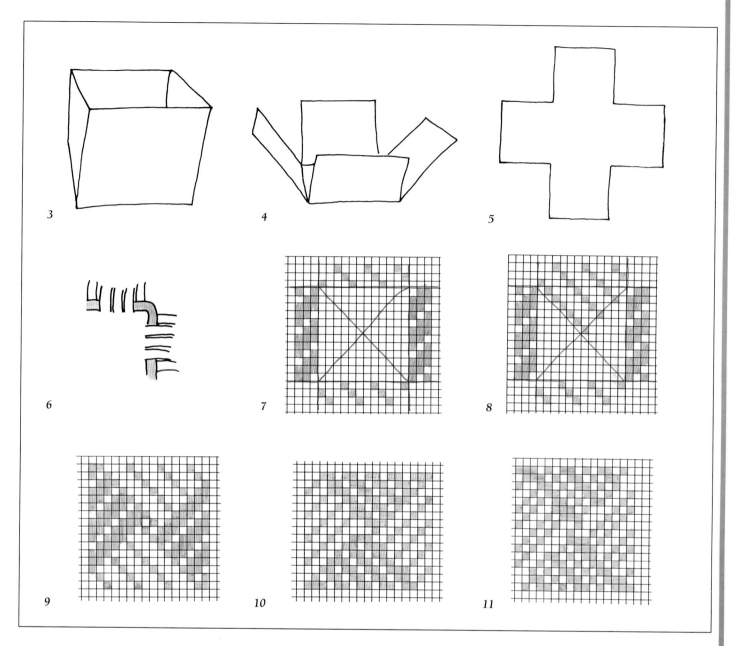

3

4

5

6

7

8

9

10

11

you're drafting a plus mark shape.

When flattened out on the draft, a row woven around the basket (on the sides) goes around the center of the plus mark. See illustration 6. Notice how the row starts by weaving horizontally then changes to a vertical weave. That transition is CRITICAL.

Because of the horizontal–vertical–horizontal–vertical aspect of each row, the draft must change from overs to unders (dark to light) with the start of each new row. If this is hard to imagine, just weave a quick sample. You'll see that it works automatically.

Illustration 7 shows a draft of the sides for an over three, under one twill. To decide how the base should be drafted, divide the base into quadrants. Yes, these are different quadrants than we've been using so far.

To draft the base, just continue the twill lines down into the quadrants. Illustration 8 shows one quadrant finished.

Illustration 9 shows the complete draft for the base, without the sides attached. Obviously these twills work better if the base is one color in both directions.

Illustration 10 is a draft of the base for another linear twill. This base sets up an over two, under one twill.

Linear twills can also have multiple lines. The base in illustration 11 sets up an over two, under one, over one, under one twill (2,1,1,1). Once you understand the flow of linear twills, you'll find you can set up whatever pattern you want. Just draft it and weave it.

Linear twills can zigzag as well as spiral, of course. To change direction, just reverse your pattern the same way you do with repeating diamonds. Refer to the "Basic Diamonds" chapter if you are unsure of the technique.

Above left: "The Original Fibonacci" by Billie Ruth Sudduth. Flat oval and half-round reed, natural and commercially dyed, 9" x 9" x 12", 1991. Photo: Melva Calder.

Above right: "Pottery V" by Carol-Ann Stentiford. Continuous pattern weaving. Black walnut and tobacco-dyed reed, 12" x 11" dia., 1991. Photo: Carol-Ann Stentiford.

Right: "Pottery I" by Carol-Ann Stentiford. Natural and walnut-dyed reed, 9-1/2" x 8-1/2" x 5-1/2", 1991. Photo: Carol-Ann Stentiford.

Designing Your Own Twills

Anonymous, backpack from Borneo. Sisal, reed, 16-1/2" x 10" dia., ca. 1984. Photo: Judy Mulford. From the collection of Judy Mulford.

Designing a twill is so easy, you're probably already doing it. Designing starts with little "adjustments" when you want something bigger or smaller. It can happen when you make a "samples" basket, where the base is one twill, and each side is a different twill. It can also happen when you think two twills will look good together, you try the combination, and it works.

Designing, especially as discussed in this chapter, is easiest on a piece of graph paper. Pull out your graph pad, wide felt-tip pen, bottle of correction fluid, and let's start sketching. I always keep graph paper with me to sketch what I see or to explore "what if" questions.

Note: This chapter uses diamonds for illustrations, but all of these techniques work just as easily for blocks.

BUILDING REPEAT PATTERNS

Let's start the design process by filling in a simple form, like a diamond. An empty diamond like the one in illustration 1 lacks visual interest, and the floats are too long. Fill it in with a pattern of your choice.

When using the "fill-in" method, it is wise to make several of the basic outlines on your graph paper. Some of the patterns you design will be "keepers" and some won't. If you have many outlines, you can experiment, giving you a larger selection of designs to weave.

Filling in becomes a question of how the interior space should be divided. In illustration 2, a border of plus marks forms the bottom, while a single plus mark forms the top. Play the "what if" game. How would this change if diamonds were used instead of plus marks? What if all the plus marks were light, instead of light and dark? Suppose the outline diamond were larger.

You can concentrate on each of the four corners rather than on the top and bottom. Illustration 3 shows diamonds placed in each corner, with an "X" dividing them from each other.

"What if" questions spark your imagination, asking you to look at the problem a different way. Start asking yourself ques-

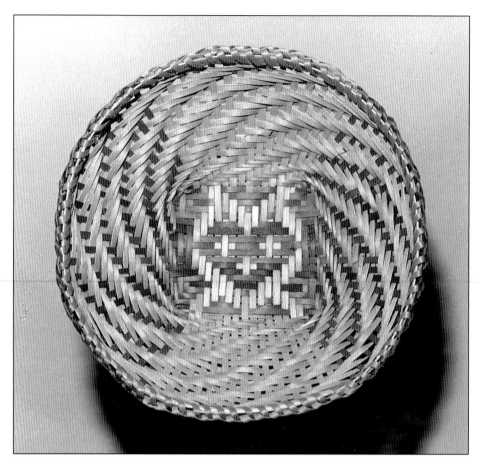

"Heart Swirl" by Joan Moore. Reed and cane, 4" x 13-1/2" dia., 1990. Photo: Dick Moore.

tions and trying out the answers on your graph paper. For example, do you need the "X" division? Would it look better if some of the diamonds were larger than others? Do the colors need to alternate?

When you start at the center, you have to be careful not to make a basic twill. One possibility is to make wide or slender diamonds inside a normal diamond (see illustration 4). Perhaps a dark space inside the light diamond would work. Or...?

If the outlined shape is enlarged as shown in illustration 5, you have more interior space to design. Starting at the bottom, this space contains a border of empty space, which is bordered with two rows of plus marks. The remainder is filled with diagonal lines.

Now that you've designed some patterned diamonds, what do you do with

them? They can be used for the center point or a single spot of interest, surrounded with a basic twill (diagonal lines). Another option is to combine them, forming a complex pattern.

Joan Moore's "Heart Swirl" uses a filled heart pattern that is very effective, and it's only used once.

Illustration 6 shows some outlines put together to form an overall pattern. This is a slightly elongated diamond, but any basic shape works.

Now fill in the outlines. In illustration 7, several different patterns are used, but a couple of patterns could be repeated several times. This type of design might make an interesting band around a basket. With all of these different patterns, this design is probably too busy to cover an entire basket. Keep that in mind when you're

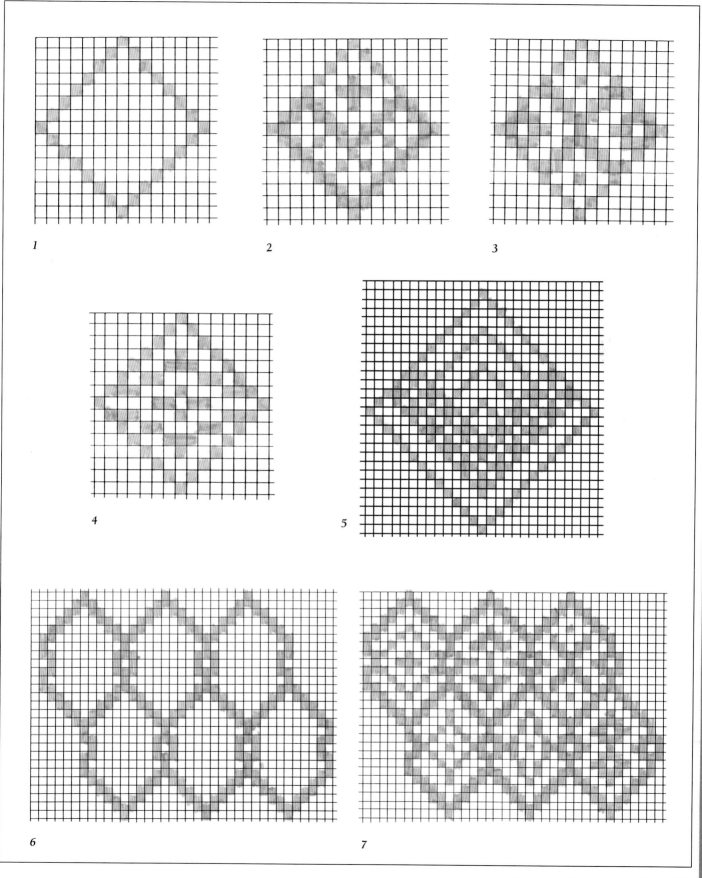

1

2

3

4

5

6

7

drafting. If the design is too complex, the viewer will decide it is too confusing. Allow the eye someplace to rest—a wide outline, one very large pattern, or lots of repeating, simple patterns.

Working with an outline is an easy way to build a complex repeating pattern. Start with a shape that interests you. In illustration 8, I've chosen a curving diamond.

Fill in the outline (illustration 9).

Make duplicates of the design, and combine them (see illustration 10). There are many patterns for combining the outlines. They can be arranged like bricks or stacked on top of themselves. A checkerboard also works, or you can stagger the outlines into diagonals (a twill of outline shapes). For more repeat pattern methods, look at some textile printing books.

Illustration 11 looks far different from the last one, but it isn't. Find the three curved diamond outlines. The empty spaces between them have been filled

Untitled by Lyn Siler. Rattan, 13" x 13" 9", 1991. Photo: Will Siler.

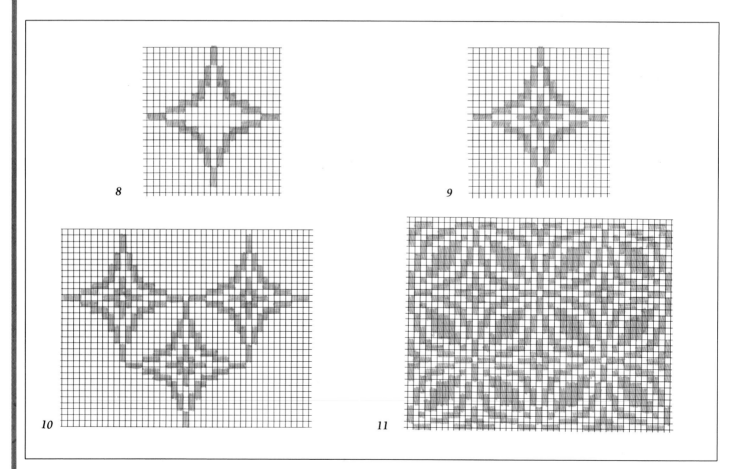

8

9

10

11

because the floats are too long if the empty spaces are left empty.

This pattern looks a lot like a colonial coverlet. Coverlets are twills, but loom weaving allows a row of very thin plain weave to be inserted between each pattern row. Some coverlet patterns demand that plain weave, and the plain weave row does not translate gracefully into basketry. Despite the fact that they do not reproduce well in basketry, coverlets can provide design inspiration.

LINES AND BORDERS

Lines are wonderful design elements and easy to work with in twill. Using graph paper, you can draw lines wherever and however you want them. Then just weave your basket according to your draft.

The five-element border shown in the Philippine wallet in the photo, and in illustration 12, is one of the most common for lines. It snakes its way around baskets all over the world. The weave must step over one in each row; otherwise, the vertical floats become too long,

Anonymous, Philippine wallet. A 3/3 twill. Bamboo, 4-1/2" x 8" x 1/2", collected mid-1980's. Photo: David LaPlantz. From the collection of David and Shereen LaPlantz.

but it can be easily modified into a curve.

Illustration 13 shows a three-element version of the above line. This border is so narrow, it can become lost in a patterned background. Consequently, it looks best when highlighted with a plain border on

each side. This line can also be modified into a curve to snake around a basket.

Based on a 3-block twill, the border in illustration 14 has a 3-block on each side of a square of floats. It, too, has to step over one for each row. However, this

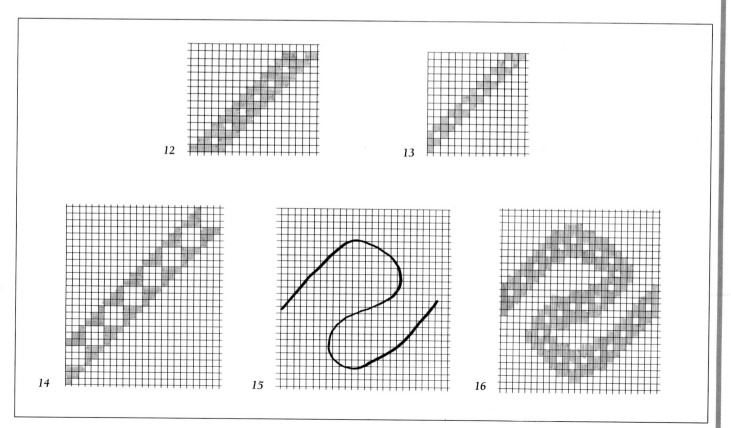

border cannot be modified into a curve.

Notice how many different borders are used to make the designs on these Chitimacha baskets. (You can also see that one has a "fake it" section on the bottom left corner.)

To make a border snake around your basket, start by drawing a snaking line on your graph paper (illustration 15). Size counts; if the elements you plan to use are the same width as your graph paper, draw the snaking line exactly the size you want on your basket. (A 5-inch-tall basket gets a 5-inch-tall draft.) If the graph's width is half the width of the element, then draw the lines half the size you want on your basket.

Next, draw your border on top of the snaking line. Illustration 16 shows a first draft. It can be used as it is, or modified to have better looking curves for the basket. To fit the curves, the two-row pattern of over five, over two, under one, over two is modified when necessary. You're the designer; you can modify it any way you want.

BACKGROUND FILL

Sometimes you'll want to have a whole area dark or light, or you may want to create a specific image or symbol. This is sometimes impossible because of float length. No matter how much you want a design, you can't use a basket with 4-inch floats sagging around it.

One solution is to tie down the floats; that means weave them. Tying down the floats shouldn't interfere with, or distract from, the main pattern. A simple twill line or random pattern generally looks unimportant, and it fades visually into the background.

Illustration 17 is just one example of simple twill lines you can use for a background pattern. These simple lines can be very effective running behind a more dramatic design.

Satin weave is the other solution for float problems. We think of satin as a fabric; actually, the fabric is named after the twill used to weave it. Satin is a broken twill, and there are many, many satin

Anonymous, Chitimacha, lidded, double-weave baskets . River cane, both 6" x 6" x 6", old. From the Delhaye collection.

patterns. (For reference purposes, some weaving books show more satin variations.)

There are mathematical formulas for each of these satin weaves, but I don't recommend that you use them. They're better suited to fabric weaving. Instead, just copy the weaves in illustrations 18 through 25.

Each weave is illustrated both as the repeat unit and as the overall pattern.

EVERYTHING AND ANYTHING IN TWILL

Anything you can draw can become a twill. The only limitation is that your images must fit onto graph paper. They look like computer bit-mapped graphics, but if you work with really thin elements, the images will appear more curved than bit-mapped.

Anonymous, Philippine lidded basket. Bamboo, 6" x 13" x 14" (with handle), contemporary. Photo: author. From the collection of David and Shereen LaPlantz.

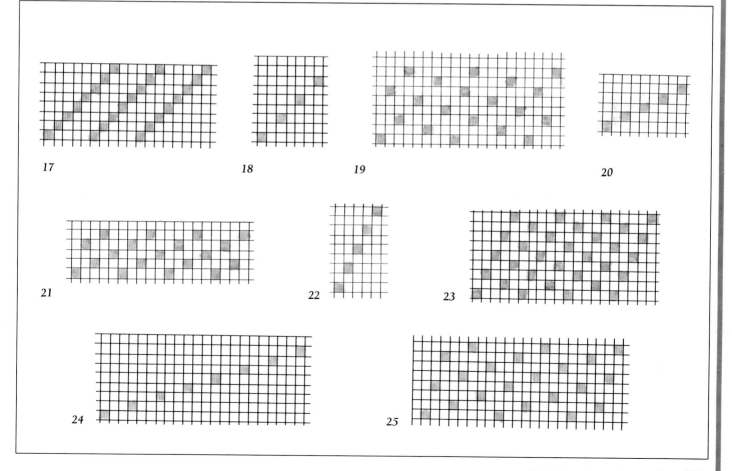

17

18

19

20

21

22

23

24

25

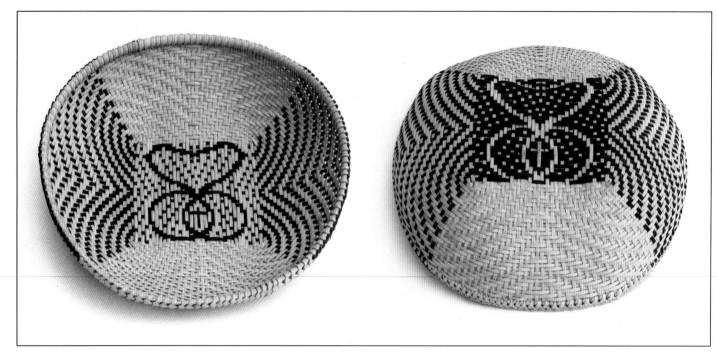

"Wedding Basket" by Patti Hawkins. A 2/2 twill. Reed, 4" x 16" dia., 1991. Photos: David LaPlantz.

Patti Hawkins' basket in these photographs was a gift commemorating a wedding. The design includes a heart, two wedding rings, and a cross. As you can see, twill lines can be woven into whatever design you want. Notice the satin weave fill. Also, because the central pattern is an unbalanced twill, it has a dark side and a light side.

To design your own twill, start by drawing whatever you want on graph paper. It doesn't have to be a simple heart (as shown in illustration 26); render your house, your child's face, or a perfect rose.

Translate that drawing into squares on the graph paper. (Fill in each of the squares that the drawing crosses as shown in illustration 27.)

Decide on a design to fill the interior space of your outline. Some suggestions are shown in illustrations 28 and 29.

Now determine how you wish the outlined shape to repeat. In illustration 30, I chose to duplicate more hearts from the center outward, like a basic twill. I could just as easily have chosen a brick, checkerboard, or stack pattern.

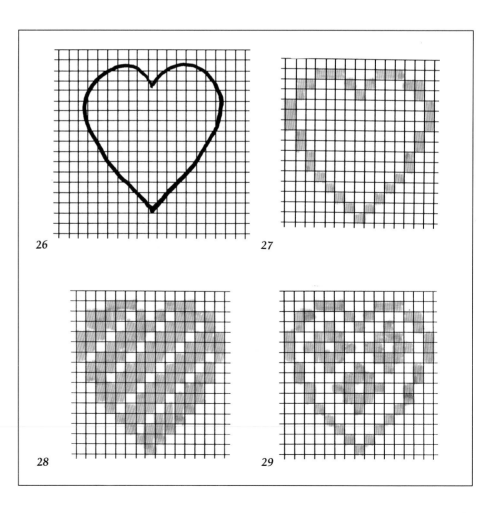

26   27

28   29

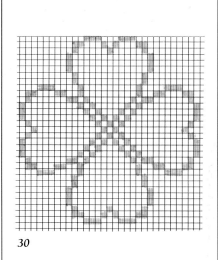

30

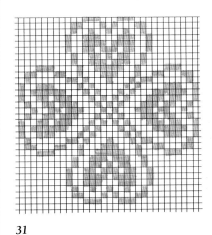

31

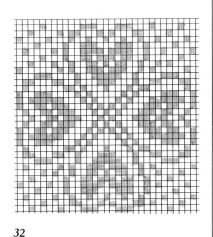

32

Anonymous, rice basket from Kalimantan, Indonesia. Bamboo, 8" high x 5-1/2" x 5-1/2" base, 11" dia. top, old. Photo: David LaPlantz. From the collection of David and Shereen LaPlantz.

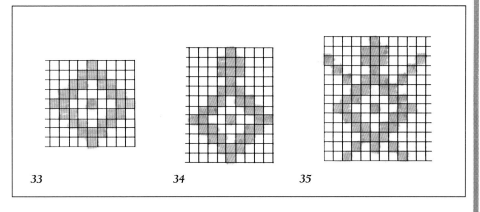

33   34   35

Once you have settled on a repeat pattern, fill in each shape. You can see by illustration 31 that I decided against the fill patterns previously illustrated and designed a whole new one.

Fill in the background with simple twill lines or satin weave (illustration 32). Now that the designing is done, decide how you want to weave it as a basket. Will this be the base, and do you want it to show? If so, the basket will have to be a tray or a shallow bowl. Otherwise, what will the sides look like? Will they replicate the base, dovetail, or simply be similar? If the sides are similar, rather than the same, you must design the sides also.

I'm serious when I say you can make anything into twills. To make that point, let's use something absurd but not too realistic. Let's make stylized bugs!

To make a stylized animal, start with something simple like a diamond. See illustration 33.

Add a head (illustration 34).

Now add some legs, and even a tail, if you want (illustration 35).

I want bugs crawling around my basket, so, instead of a regular combination

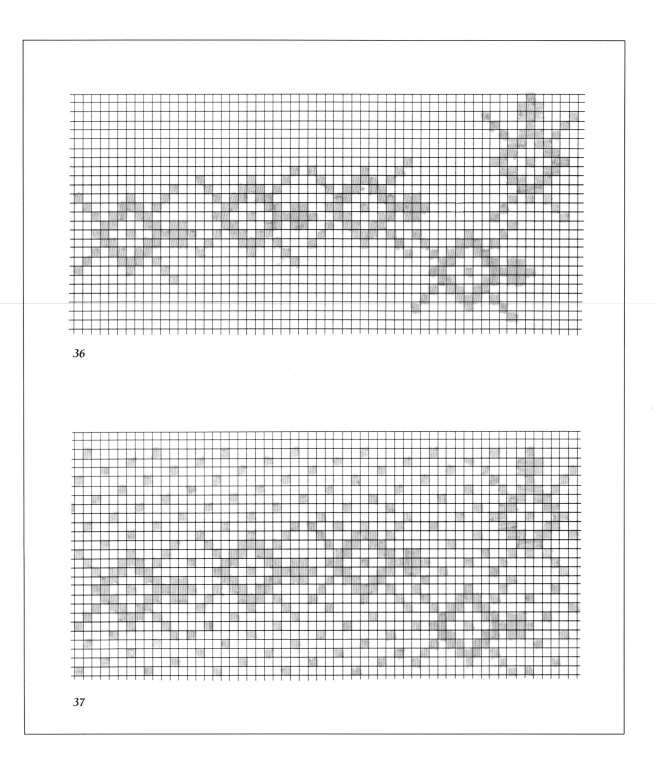

36

37

pattern, I'm scattering them across the side. For visual interest (and humor) I have one bug heading off on its own. See illustration 36.

Fill in the background with satin weave or simple twill lines (illustration 37). When you're satisfied with the design, weave the basket.

Twill is so versatile, you can write on your basket! Sign your basket in the weave, or write poetry up the side. Ask your friends for their signatures, and make a "friendship basket." There really are no limits.

Illustration 38 shows a simple alphabet you can use, and you can

design your own, more fanciful ones.

Keep in mind that the sides and the base do not have to be the same. The photographs on the next page show an Indonesian rice basket with three different sides (one is repeated) and a different base. Be careful not to get too complicated or confusing, but also try not to be boring.

Anonymous, lidded basket from Lom Bok, Indonesia. A 2/2 twill with "Lom Bok" written across lid. Bamboo, 9" x 11" x 1-1/2", contemporary. Photo: author. From the collection of David and Shereen LaPlantz.

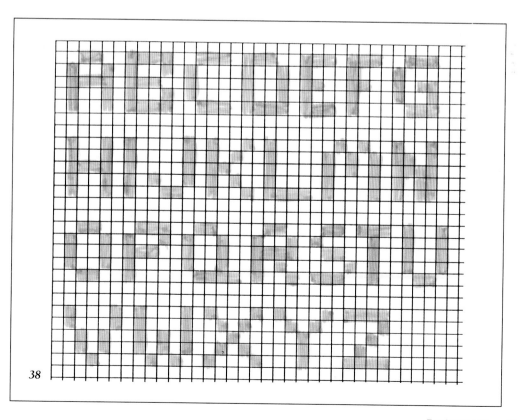

38

Anonymous, rice basket, Kalimantan, Indonesia.
Bamboo, 8-1/2" high x 7" x 7" base, 12" dia. top,
old. Photos: David LaPlantz. From the collection
of David and Shereen LaPlantz.

Undulating Twills

Twills are quite beautiful when woven in the ordinary fashion, using elements that are all the same width. They become much more exciting if the widths are varied. That makes the twills undulate.

Untitled by Judith Olney. Double, undulating twill. Reed, 15" x 13" x 9", 1991. Photo: Roger Olney.

Undulating Twills

Illustrations 1 and 2 are a reminder of the basic diamond and basic "X" twill. Remember what they look like because they'll change radically when the width of their elements starts to vary.

The same basic diamond and "X" twills are shown in illustrations 3 and 4, but here their elements vary in width both vertically and horizontally. The width pattern is 1–1–1–1–1–2–2–2–3–3–5–3–3–2–2–2–repeat. (Translation: One means one unit or width. Two means twice as wide as one. Three is three times as wide as one, and five is five times as wide. Repeat starting with one again.)

IMPORTANT: Place the widest elements wherever you're going to change direction (turn a corner, upstake, etc.). If a corner is turned on a narrow element, the tension can be very hard to handle.

There are two ways to cause pattern changes in undulating twills. One is to change the pattern of widths by altering the numbers. If the last pattern was 1–1–1–2–2–, try a new one that's 1–2–3–2–; they'll look radically different. The second way is to keep the same pattern of widths and change the twill.

Illustrations 5 and 6 show the same two basic twills, the diamond and the "X," in a different width pattern: 2–2–1–1–1–2–2–4–3–1–3–4–2–2–1–1–1–repeat.

The width pattern can have any variations you want. The only limitations are the two obvious ones: availability of your material in all the desired widths, and float length.

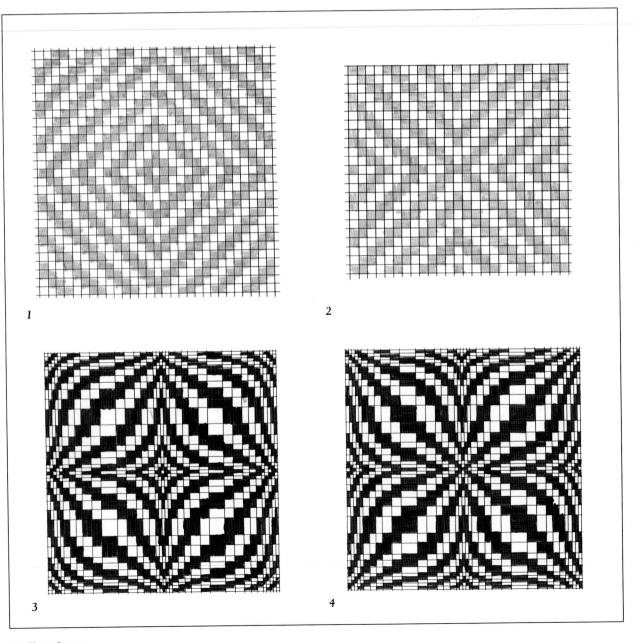

1

2

3

4

5

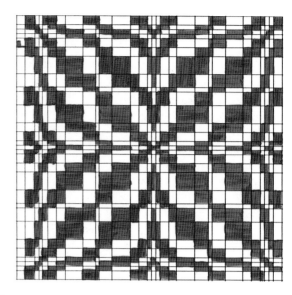

6

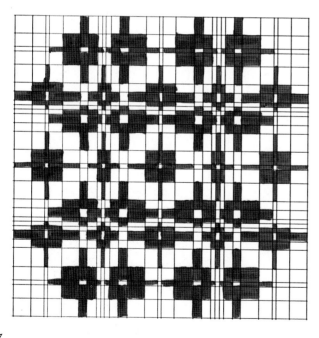

7

8

Illustration 7 has the same width pattern used for the last two illustrations, but the twill pattern is different. This is the center unit for diamonds dovetailed like a brick wall.

The diamond pattern used for the last illustration is shown in a different width pattern in illustration 8. Here it is 4–3–2–1–2–3–4–5–repeat.

The pattern in illustration 9 changes everything. The twill is two sizes of a basic diamond with a few rows surrounding each diamond. The width pattern is 1–1–1–1–1–2–2–2–3–3–5–3–2–2–1–1–1–2–2–3–5–3–3–2–2–2–repeat.

The twill patterns don't have to be basic. Illustration 10 shows a design using double-ended arrows. In illustration 11, it is drafted in the same width pattern as the one used in illustration 9.

The widths don't have to vary in both directions. As you can see by comparing the samples in the photographs, varying the widths in only one direction radically alters the appearance.

If you choose to vary the widths in both directions, you can use one width pattern for the verticals and a different pattern for the horizontals. (Combine that with a complex twill, and it's beyond my imagination, but it could be wonderful!)

TIP: Although it's an interesting experience (miracle?) to make an undulating twill without drafting it first, I find drafting helps. Of course, the stationery store doesn't carry graph paper in your favorite width variations, so you have to make your own. I've used two different methods to make graph paper, and both work. The first is to take existing graph paper (with very small squares) and draw new lines on it wherever desired. This is a very quick way to sketch something. Sometimes I don't even use a ruler; I just make fast and sloppy lines. The other method is to draw graph paper on the computer. It takes a bit longer, looks much nicer, and when I want a second piece of that graph paper, all I have to do is push "print."

NON-UNDULATING WIDTH CHANGES

Finally, the width pattern can be random. The artist who crafted the lidded basket on page 122 obviously tried for a regular, even pattern with uniform elements, but the material came in a variety of widths. Because the elements were used at random, the lines don't undulate, they wiggle across the basket.

Elements can also be split to change the pattern appearance. Each element can be split in half or smaller widths. According to the desires of the artist, the elements can be split in half at one point and, further on, split again.

9

10

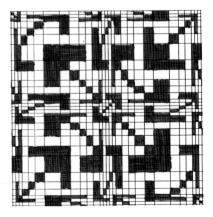

11

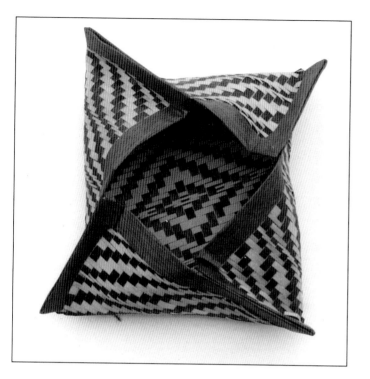

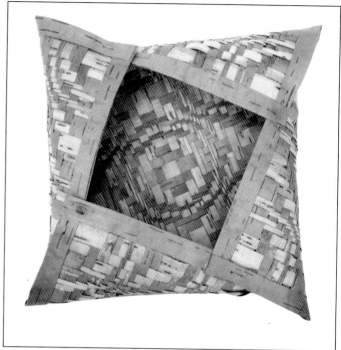

Untitled sample by author. Basic diamond with width variation in one direction. Top: folded. Bottom: before folding. Photos: David LaPLantz.

Untitled sample by author. Basic diamond with width variation in both directions. Top: folded. Bottom: before folding. Photos: David LaPlantz.

Right: Anonymous, lidded basket, probably southeast Asia. A 4-block twill. Lauhala, 9" x 10" x 3-1/2", contemporary. Photo: David LaPlantz.

Below: Anonymous, Yap baby basket, Micronesia. Plaited twill and braiding. Pandanus, coconut husk fiber, 39" x 5-1/2" x 12", 1990. Photo: Judy Mulford. From the collection of Judy Mulford.

Double Weave

Double weave always sounds hard, but it isn't. It's just tedious, because you have to make two baskets to get one.

To make a double weave basket, cut elements twice as long as you would normally. Start by weaving the inside base; then weave up the sides, turn, and weave back down on the outside, using the interior basket as a mold. Lastly, weave across the bottom. All of the elements naturally develop partners and thread down their partner's weave (throat). Clip off the excess, and you're finished.

In twill, I frequently see the interior basket woven out of wide elements that are split near the top. That makes the exterior weave finer and lovelier. Let's look at some double weave twill baskets.

This Mexican basket is shallow, allowing the interior to show. It weaves from the inside out, and the twill is continued on the exterior sides. The artist obviously wanted to finish quickly and left the floats on the exterior base quite long. The weaving in the center of the base holds everything in place and allows a few elements to be tucked into the weave securely. You

can see that the other elements are tucked under the long floats, possibly tucked into the weave of the interior base. (Otherwise, they would have worked loose long ago.)

This Tarahumara basket is also woven from the inside to the outside. The palm leaves are only used on the exterior weaving. Notice that the inside base is a 4-block, changing quickly to an over two, under two twill, but the exterior base is a 6-block twill. I assume size had less to do with the change than finishing easily.

Why do all the work of double weave and not highlight that work? Don't let

Left: Anonymous, Mexico, interior and bottom. Banana, 7" x 7" x 3-1/2", contemporary. Photos: author. From the collection of David and Shereen LaPlantz.

Right: Anonymous, Tarahumara tribe from northern Mexico, interior and bottom. Pine needle and palm, 3" x 4" dia., contemporary. From the collection of Kathy Dannerbeck.

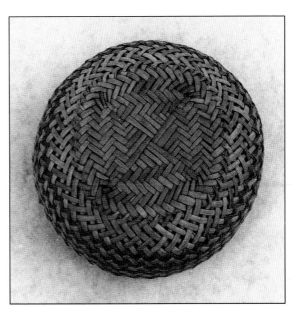

Double Weave

your audience miss your efforts. Sosse Baker's baskets use twill patterns effectively to highlight the double weave. In "Inside Out," the lines spiral from the inside out, and the sides are not molded to each other. It is simple, but quite effective.

Finally, here is a wild, double weave basket, found at a flea market. It has a fun, decorative method of turning to weave the exterior sides. The exterior sides bulge because they're made with plain weave. Remember, plain weave takes up more space than twill. That fact was used effectively to create a shape for this basket. The base and the top are narrower because they are twill.

Right: "Inside Out" by Sosse Baker. A 1-2-3 continuous twill. Reed, 9" x 9" dia., 1991. Photo: Sosse Baker.

Below: Anonymous, basket vase, exterior and interior (showing double-layer base). A 2-block twill. Bamboo, 6-1/2" x 3" dia. at top. Photos: David LaPlantz.

Fun Shapes

Any shape that you can plait in plain weave, you can also plait in twill. Since this isn't a shaping book, I won't go into how to weave specific forms. Just combine twills with the shapes you already

Untitled baskets by Tom Colvin. Louisiana Choctaw-style bull nose, elbow, and cow nose shapes in various twills. River cane, bull nose: 5-1/2" x 7" x 3", early 1980's.

know, or learn some new shapes that you want to make in twill.

Don't limit yourself to simple shapes; anything goes. Let these photos tempt you into making wild, fun basket shapes!

SQUARE-ON-SQUARE BASKET

Illustration 1 shows the pattern I chose for the wall basket, or pocket, in the photograph. Since this basket does not turn any bias corners, it can be either a diamond or a block twill. A square-on-square basket is also the first step for making elbow and cow nose baskets.

Earlier I mentioned that if you have any problems with tension, weave a couple of rows of plain weave. For this basket I needed the plain weave to help with tension at the "turn" edges. Three rows of plain weave are also used at the top to make a fold and tuck rim. (You can make a neater rim if you use four rows of plain weave, however.)

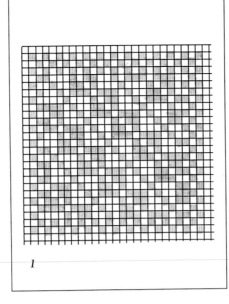

1

Right: Untitled by author, front and back. A 2/2, 1-block (or broken-diamond) twill. Microwood, 6" x 9" x 2", 1991. Photos: David LaPlantz.

BULL NOSE BASKET

These photographs show the front and back of the same bull nose basket. Notice that the patterns appear to be radically different. On the back, bias plaiting results in a color plaid, so I made pattern breaks on the front to create a pattern plaid. The weave is shown in illustration 2.

You can put pattern breaks wherever you want them. Make this row opposite the last, and it's a pattern break. If there are pattern breaks in the base, there are automatically pattern breaks in the sides.

TIP: When weaving a complex shape, sometimes the pattern just won't work. It's frustrating, and you may be tempted to force the weave. Relax; this impossible situation is telling you that a pattern break is needed.

Left: Untitled wall pocket by author. A 3-block twill. Microwood, 7" x 7", 1991. Photo: David LaPlantz.

Two other styles of bull noses are represented in the work of Tom Colvin and an unknown artist from Sri Lanka. They are woven with straight, rather than bias sides.

Anonymous, Sri Lanka. Bull nose in 2/2 twill. Bamboo, 6" x 6" x 4", contemporary. Photo: author.

Untitled by Tom Colvin. Louisiana Choctaw-style, bull nose in 3/3 twill. River cane, 5-1/2" x 7" x 3", 1983. Photo: author.

JUXTAPOSED SQUARES

This basket has a square base and a square top, but, because the squares are opposite each other (juxtaposed), the sides

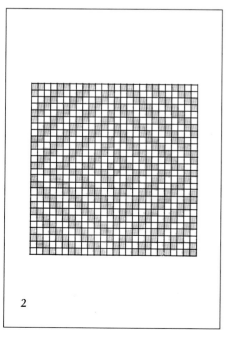

Untitled by author. A 3-block twill. Microwood, 9" x 9" x 6", 1992. Photo: author.

2

are automatically forced into triangles. Notice how the pattern actually goes up one side, over the shoulder, and down the next side. (The pattern is shown in illustration 3.) Twill really does wrap around corners and edges!

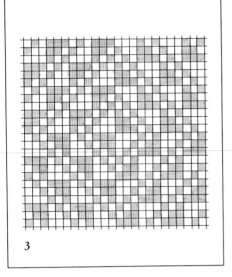

3

Untitled by author. Block twill variation. Microwood, 7" x 4" x 5", 1992. Photo: David LaPlantz.

W-FOOT BASKET

This basket has two bias corners on a side, an "impossibility" which results in a distorted, W-shaped base. Here the pattern wraps around the sides, causing squares on the edges as well as on the sides. Refer to illustration 4 for the pattern draft.

Twill in exotic shapes is incredible. This is just the smallest taste of what can happen. When you're comfortable with twill, take a shaping workshop, or get a shaping book, like my *Plaited Folios*, and go crazy. Discover how each pattern looks wrapping around those strange corners and edges.

VARIATION— "NECKING IN"

This isn't an exotic shape, but it is a shaping option to remember. The basket is a basic over two, under two twill. To "neck in," the artist simply took two elements and pretended they were one. It was an arbitrary decision. As you can see in the photograph, there is suddenly half as much weaving as before. The floats look a bit longer, but by the time everything settles in place, the basket has a smaller opening.

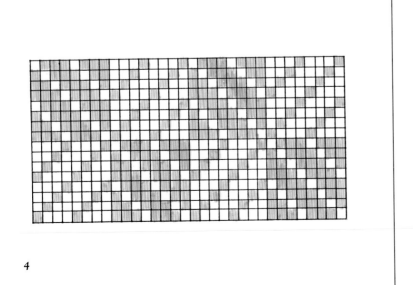

4

RIB-CONSTRUCTION TWILL

Twill doesn't have to be plaited; it can also be woven. Here twill is used in rib-construction basketry. If you were to look at a draft of this pattern, it would look distorted, but the uneven spacing creates a pleasing effect in the basket.

Left top: Anonymous, probably Philippine. A 2/2, 3-block. Bamboo, 9-1/2" x 9-1/2" x 9", contemporary. Photo: author. From the collection of David and Shereen LaPlantz.

Bottom: Untitled by Betty Kemink. Reed and vine, 18" x 27" x 5", 1991. Photo: Jerry Kemink.

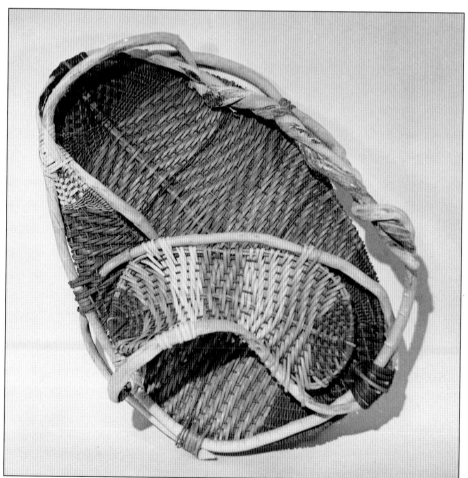

PARTING THOUGHTS

We have sat together, through the chapters of this book, sharing much of what makes twill special. Take what you have learned, and try whatever aspects of twill excite and intrigue you. Develop each pattern that you care about, and—above all—trust in your heart. If you do things that you love, that love will show in your work. If you only do things that you "should," your work will reflect that too.

My most exciting baskets, the ones that burst with personality, are the ones I make spontaneously for friends to say "congratulations" or "thank you." Those baskets have no "shoulds"—they're pure "me."

My wish for you is that twill will become part of your expression of yourself. I hope that twill, with all of its variations, excites you, and that your baskets will reflect that excitement.

BASIC PLAITING

This section provides step-by-step instructions on how to plait. If you have never plaited a basket before, please follow these directions, and plait several baskets before you attempt twill. Trying anything for the first time is difficult; if we try to learn two or three new things at once, it's even harder. Make it easy on yourself, and go one step at a time. Plait first; then plait twill.

Plaiting is the same as weaving in every respect but one—tension. Plaited tension is equidistant in all directions; i.e., all of the elements are evenly spaced. In weaving, the stakes are spaced apart, and the weavers are packed closely together.

There are two types of plaiting, straight and bias. In straight plaiting, the elements are woven perpendicular to the base; in bias plaiting, they weave at a 45° angle.

STRAIGHT PLAITING

With the center portion of each element, use an over one, under one pattern (plain weave) to plait a base as shown in illustration 1. Adjust the tension frequently, making sure that everything is evenly spaced. Hold everything securely in place with clothespins at the corners and along the sides.

As shown in illustration 2, fold all of the elements up sharply, around the outside edge of the base (upstake).

Using a new, separate element, weave a row around the basket. Be sure to maintain the over one, under one pattern (see illustration 3). Overlap the ends by about four stakes (uprights) or 2 inches. Clip off

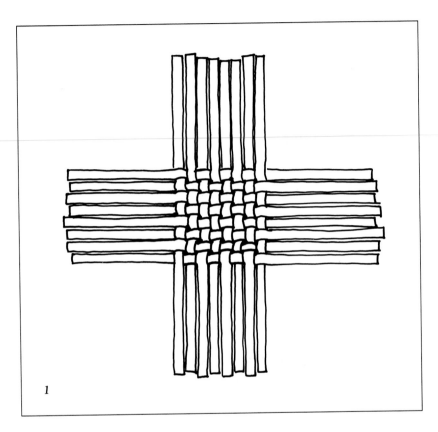

1

any excess.

If you tilt the base, as shown in illustration 4, you can see that the over one, under one pattern is maintained around the edge. Check yours before going on to the next row.

Use a new element to weave each row around the basket (illustration 5). Overlap the ends, and clip off the excess. Be sure to rotate the sides to begin each row. Adjust the tension frequently, and use lots of clothespins to hold everything in place.

When the basket is exactly the way you want it, make the rim. For a lashed rim (also called a sandwich and sew), fold all of the inside elements to the outside. Trim them to about seven-eighths of the width of the top row. See illustration 6.

Now fold all of the outside elements to the inside, and trim them like the others (illustration 7).

Wrap two elements around the top, "sandwiching" the top row (illustration 8). Secure everything in place with clothespins.

Whip stitch the "sandwiching" elements in place (illustration 9).

Another option is to make a fold and tuck rim. For this rim, the unwoven portion of the elements must be long enough to tuck into the weave. See illustration 10.

First fold all of the inside elements to the outside. Tuck them into the weave at the first opportunity (third row), and clip off any excess (illustration 11).

Next fold all of the outside elements to the inside. At the first opportunity (again the third row), tuck them into the weave (illustration 12). Clip off any excess.

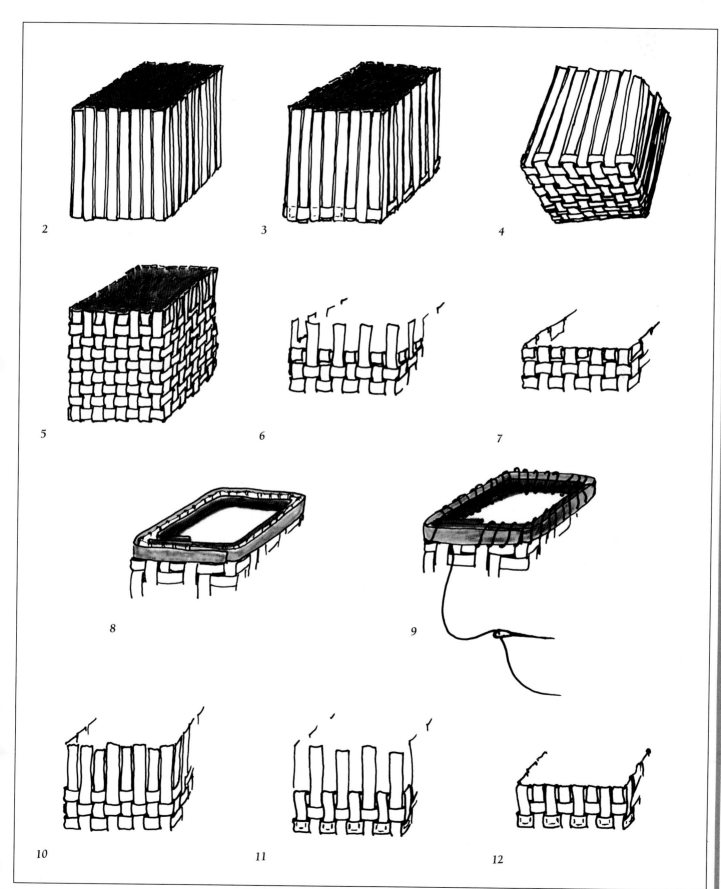

2

3

4

5

6

7

8

9

10

11

12

Basic Plaiting

BIAS PLAITING

Using an even number of elements in each direction, plait a base just as you did for straight plaiting (illustration 13). Bias plaiting consumes more material than straight plaiting, and to make a basket of equivalent size, you must start with elements that are about one-third longer.

Pick any side, and divide that side in half. Now fold the two halves across each other as shown in illustration 14. The two halves weave together to form the sides of the basket. That is why you must have an even number of elements and start with longer elements.

As shown in illustration 15, weave the first row across in each direction. The over one, under one pattern is maintained.

Continue weaving the rest of the elements across each other, adjusting the

tension frequently. (See illustration 16.) When there are no more elements to weave, you're done with one side. This is a "bias corner." Repeat the above steps on all four sides.

Notice that the ends from one bias corner overlap the ends from the adjacent bias corner. (Refer to illustration 17.) Every time you find elements overlapping, weave them, continuing the same pattern until you reach the top.

You've reached the top when there's

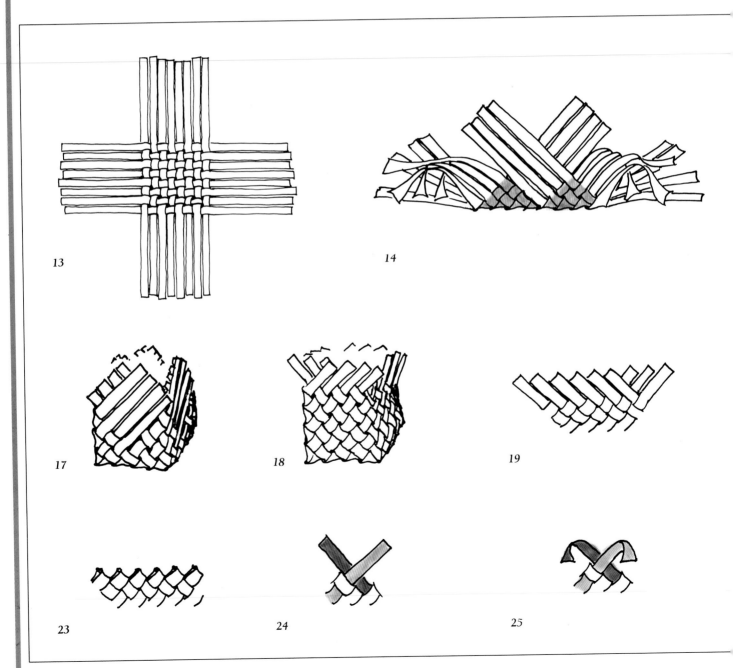

13

14

17

18

19

23

24

25

nothing more to weave (illustration 18).

Find a row of "over ones" around the top of your basket (see illustration 19). These will become your rim. Again, before starting the rim, make sure the basket is exactly the way you want it to look.

As highlighted in illustration 20, select two elements, one in each direction, that form an "X."

For a serrated rim, fold the inside element to the outside. Tuck it into the weave at the first opportunity as shown in illustration 21.

Fold the other element to the outside, locking in the first, and tuck it into the weave at the first opportunity. See illustration 22.

Repeat around the basket (illustration 23); then clip off any excess.

To make a straight, or flat rim, start the same way. Select two elements that make an "X." (See illustration 24)

Fold both elements forward as a unit (illustration 25).

Tuck each element into its partner's weave. The left-most drawing in illustration 26 shows each element tucking into the first opportunity; the other example allows one element to tuck into the second opportunity. They both work, but have different appearances.

Whichever style you use, repeat it around the basket (illustration 27). Then clip off any excess.

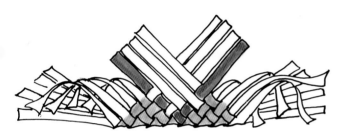

15

16

20

21

22

26

27

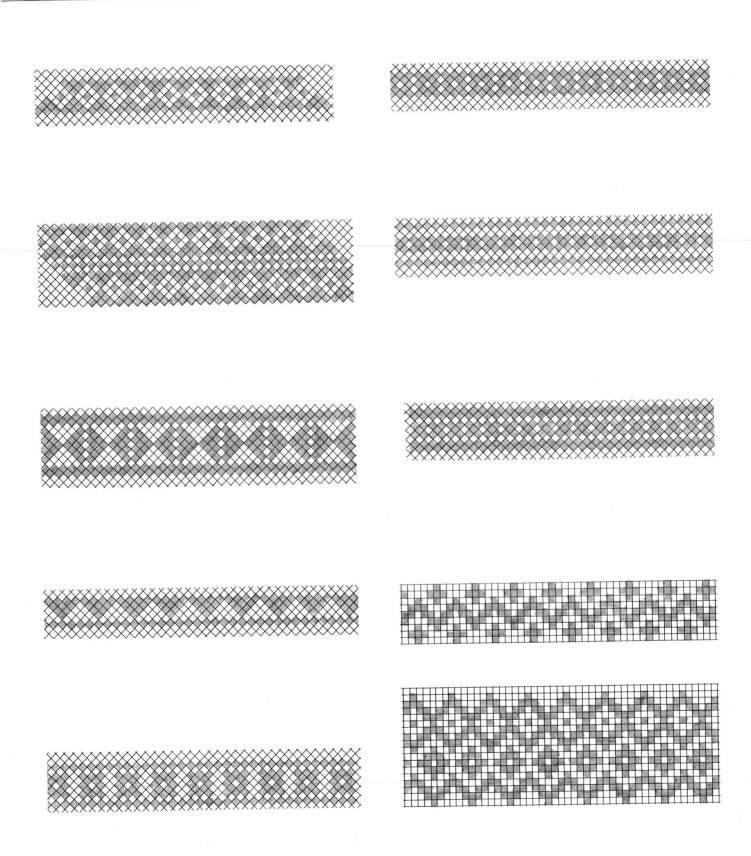

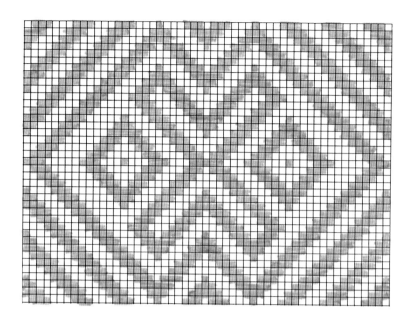

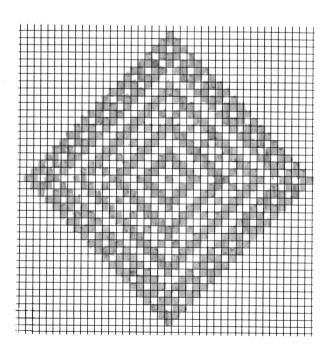

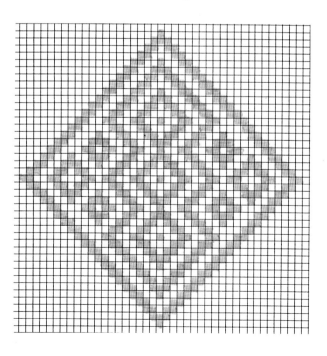

Left: Anonymous, Philippines. Twill with satin weave. Bamboo, 4" x 4" x 6", contemporary. Photo: author.

Below: Untitled by Judith Olney. Double, undulating quatrefoil. Reed, 9-1/2" x 12" dia., 1991. Photo: Roger Olney.

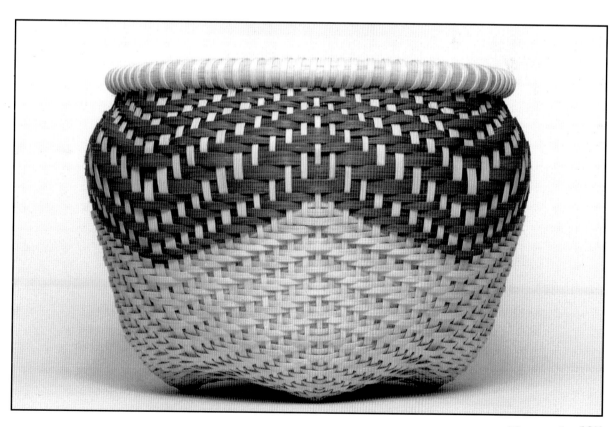

Photographs

Top left: Anonymous, purse from Suva, Fiji. Natural and dyed pandanus, 8" x 3" x 5-1/2", 1990. Photo: Judy Mulford. From the collection of Judy Mulford.

Right: Anonymous, Chinese wedding basket. Twill and open weave. Bamboo, 36" x 14" dia., contemporary. Photo: author.

Bottom left: Anonymous, purse, Suva, Fiji. Natural and dyed pandanus, 14" x 4" x 10-1/2", 1990. Photo: Judy Mulford. From the collection of Judy Mulford.

Right: Anonymous, carrying basket, Suva, Fiji. Double-woven, plaited twill. Pandanus, natural and dyed, 18" x 11" x 14", 1991. Photo: July Mulford. From the collection of Judy Mulford.

Top left: "Cherokee-Patterned Hamper" by Joyce Schaum. Rattan reed, 17" x 17" x 24", 1991. Photo: Gary Schaum.

Right: "Drury Lane" by Susi Nuss. Diamond twill. Black ash splints, shagbark hickory handle and rims, 12" x 12" x 12", 1991. Photo: Susi Nuss.

Bottom: "Basara I, II" by Keiko Takeda. Flat rattan and copper, I—20" x 6" x 12", II—15" x 6" x 16", 1992.

Statistics

If you would like to make some of the sample baskets presented in this book, vital statistics are given below for your convenience.

Basic Diamonds

page 26 (bottom)
Sherry O'Connor
2/2 diamond twill
watercolor paper, 1/4" wide
exterior = dark green and aqua
interior = peach and tangerine
4-1/2" x 4-1/2" x 3-1/2"
base elements = 15" long
base = 17 elements across 17 elements
sides = 13 rows high

page 30
Shereen LaPlantz
2/2 diamond twill
microwood, 1/4" wide
5-1/2" x 5-1/2" x 6"
base elements = 21" long
base = 21 elements across 21 elements
sides = 22 rows high
(Notice how thin a single element rim feels.)

page 31 (left)
Shereen LaPlantz
2/2 diamond twill
microwood, 1/4" wide
5-1/2" x 5-1/2" x 7"
base elements = 23" long
base = 21 elements across 21 elements
sides = 27 rows high
(Notice how much more substantial a wider rim
    appears.)

page 31 (right)
Shereen LaPlantz
2/2 diamond twill
flat reed, 1/4" wide
6-1/2" x 6-1/2" x 3-1/2"
base elements = 16" long
base = 25 elements across 25 elements
sides = 14 rows high

page 33
Shereen LaPlantz
2/2 diamond twill
microwood, 1/4" wide
10-1/4" x 6-1/4" x 3-3/4"
base elements = 17" or 21" long
base = 39 elements across 23 elements
sides = 13 rows high
(Notice the uneven feel of a fold and tuck rim.)

Basic Blocks

page 36
Shereen LaPlantz
4/4 4-block twill
flat reed, 1/4" wide
7" x 7" x 3-1/2"
base elements = 23" long
base = 40 elements across 40 elements
sides = 20 rows high

page 39
Shereen LaPlantz
4/4 4-block twill
flat oval reed, 1/4" wide
10" x 10" x 3"
base elements = 20" long
base = 40 elements across 40 elements
sides = 8 rows high

page 40
Shereen LaPlantz
3/3 3-block twill
space dyed ash, from 3/16" to 3/8" wide
6" x 6" x 5"
base elements = 26" long
base = 30 elements across 30 elements
sides = 24 rows high

page 41
Shereen LaPlantz
3/3 3-block twill
flat reed
base elements = 3/8" wide
side elements = 3/4" wide
12" x 12" x 1-1/2"
base elements = 19" long
base = 42 elements across 42 elements
sides = 2 rows high

page 42 (left)
Shereen LaPlantz
2/2 2-block twill
microwood, 1/4" wide
6" x 6" x 5"
base elements = 26" long
base = 32 elements across 32 elements
sides = 14 rows high

page 42 (right)
Shereen LaPlantz
2/2 2-block twill
microwood, 1/4" wide
6-1/2" x 6-1/2" x 7"
base elements = 24" long
base = 24 elements across 24 elements
sides = 27 rows high

page 43
Sherry O'Connor
2/2 2-block rectangle
flat reed, 1/4" wide
3" x 4-1/2" x 3-1/2"
base elements = 18" long
base = 16 elements across 16 elements
sides = 9 rows high
(half of each element stained for color pattern on
    sides)

page 44 (left)
Sherry O'Connor
2/2 2-block rectangle
gift wrapping paper and newspaper, 1/4" folded
2-1/4" x 3-3/4" x 3-1/4"
base elements = 14" long
base = 16 elements across 16 elements
sides = 8 rows high

page 44 (right)
Sherry O'Connor
2/2 2-block
flat reed, 1/4" wide
5-1/4" x 5-1/4" x 4-1/2"
base elements = 17" long
base = 16 elements across 16 elements
sides = 15 rows high
(base woven for bias rectangle, but basket is straight
    plaited)

page 45 (left)
Sherry O'Connor
2/2 1-block, or broken diamond twill
flat reed, 1/4" wide
4-1/2" x 4-1/2" x 7-1/4"
base elements = 22" long
base = 14 elements across 14 elements
sides = 24 rows high

page 45 (right)
Sherry O'Connor
2/1 1-block, or broken diamond twill
flat reed, 1/4" wide
3" x 3" x 5-3/4"
base elements = 22" long
base = 12 elements across 12 elements
sides = 16 rows high

page 46 (left)
Sherry O'Connor
2/1 1-block, or broken diamond twill
microwood, 1/4" wide, lined with Mi Teintes paper
3-3/4" x 3-3/4" x 3-1/2"–7"
base elements = 22" long
base = 18 elements across 18 elements
sides = 12 rows high to 23 rows high

page 46 (right)
Sherry O'Connor
2/2 1-block, or broken diamond twill
watercolor paper, 1/4" wide
3" x 3" x 2"–7"
base elements = 22" long
base = 14 elements across 14 elements
sides = 5 rows high to 20 rows high

page 47 (left)
Sherry O'Connor
2/2 1-block, or broken diamond twill
braided bamboo, about 1/2" wide
4-1/4" x 4-1/4" x 6"
base elements = 25" long
base = 10 elements across 10 elements
sides = 9 rows high
(half of each element stained for color pattern on sides)

Folded Baskets

page 53
Shereen LaPlantz
3-block twill
microwood, 1/4" wide
10" x 10" x 3-1/2"
base elements = 19" long
base = 30 elements across 30 elements
arms = 18 elements across 30 elements
(woven as a "plus mark," folded and sewn into a basket)

Glossary

Balanced twill: Weaving over and under the same number of elements, like over two and under two, or over three and under three. Balanced twills are slightly stronger than unbalanced ones, and it's easier to maintain an even tension when making them.

Bias plaiting: Weaving on a 45° angle, making "X's." The elements are uniformly spaced for an even tension.

Block twill: A twill pattern whose center is composed of four rotating units. The units are formed by a series of floats of descending lengths. For example, a 3-block has a descending pattern of 3, 2, 1.

Center unit: A single, non-repeating design component occurring in the center of a twill pattern.

Continuous pattern: A pattern that repeats (continues) around the basket.

Diamond twill: A twill pattern that forms a diamond or repeating diamonds. Because diamonds have points, this twill is always composed of an odd number of elements.

Draft: The representation, on graph paper, of a weave pattern.

Floats: The "overs" in the weave. Float length must always be considered when designing twills; a float that's too long can easily snag.

Herringbone: A twill that forms up and down points, like a series of "M's" and "W's."

Increment: The number of elements by which a pattern naturally increases. Calculate the increment by adding "overs" to "unders." For a linear twill of over three, under one, the increment is four. With a complex pattern of over two, under one, over one, under two, the increment is six. For many basic, balanced twills (like over two, under two), the increment can be halved (from four to two).

Overall design: A pattern that covers the entire basket or object. This can be a small pattern that repeats to cover the basket, or a single, huge pattern.

Pattern area: A spot of pattern within a larger area of plain weave or simple twill.

Pattern break: Where the woven pattern abruptly stops and reverses itself, creating a mirror image. This happens at the same place for each row, forming a line of pattern breaks.

Plaiting: *

Repeat pattern: A small pattern unit that is used again and again throughout the basket.

Rim: The top edge (or lip) of the basket. Rims must be sturdy, perhaps reinforced, because they suffer the most routine abrasion.

Stakes: The uprights (vertical elements) in the basket.

Straight plaiting: Weaving with verticals and horizontals (as opposed to bias weaving) with an evenly spaced tension.

Twill: Weaving over or under more than one, and starting each new row one step over to one side. Twills create an overall, diagonal pattern.

Unbalanced twill: A twill in which the "overs" are not the same as the "unders," such as over three and under one. Unbalanced twills have a stronger linear quality, but they are slightly less sturdy than balanced twills. Also, it's a bit more difficult to maintain an even tension with unbalanced twills.

Upstake: Turning up each element around the base of the basket. This establishes the basket's sides.

Warp: A weaver's term for stakes.

Weavers: The horizontal elements in the basket.

Weaving: *

Weft: A term used in weaving for the horizontal elements.

2/2—3/3—4/4: A quick method of indicating the "overs" and "unders" in a weave. A 2/2 twill indicates a weave of over two, under two. For a 3/1 twill, the pattern is over three, under one, and a 1/2 twill is over one, under two.

*Plaiting versus Weaving: The terms are often used interchangeably; both can be used for a plain over one, under one, and both can make twill. Structurally, each has two sets of elements coming together at right angles. Only the tension is different. A woven tension has stakes spaced apart and weavers packed closely together. A plaited tension is even; all of the elements are evenly spaced.

"Harukaze" by Jiro Yonezawa. Bamboo, cedar root and cane, approx. 6-2/3" x 8", 1991. Photo: Toshihiko Shibata.

"Ginkgo" by Dorothy Gill Barnes. Twill with overlays. Ginkgo bark and branches, 15" x 11" x 13", 1991. Photo: Doug Wilson.

GENERAL REFERENCE:

Gettys, Marshall. *Basketry of Southeastern Indians.* Idabel, OK: Museum of the Red River, 1984.

Harvey, Virginia I. *The Techniques of Basketry.* Seattle: University of Washington Press, 1986.

James, George Wharton. *Indian Basketry and How to Make Baskets.* Glorieta, NM: Rio Grande Press, 1903 and 1975.

Lane, Robert F. *Philippine Basketry: An Appreciation.* Manila: Bookmark, 1986.

Larsen, Jack Lenor, and Betty Freudenheim. *Interlacing: The Elemental Fabric.* Tokyo: Kodansha International, 1986.

Mason, Otis Tufton. *Aboriginal American Indian Basketry.* Santa Barbara, CA: Peregrine Smith, 1976.

Olney, Judith. *Choctaw Diagonal Twill Plaiting.* Westland, MI: MKS Publications, 1990.

Pendergrast, Mick. *Feathers and Fibre: A Survey of Traditional and Contemporary Maori Craft.* Auckland, New Zealand: Penguin Books, 1984.

———. *Raranga Whakairo: Maori Plaiting Patterns.* Auckland, New Zealand: Coromandel, 1984.

Roth, Walter Edmund. "An Introductory Study of The Arts, Crafts and Customs of the Guiana Indians." In *38th Annual Report of the Bureau of American Ethnology 1916-1917.* Washington: GPO, 1924.

Tod, Osma Gallinger. *Earth Basketry.* New York: Crown Publishers, 1972.

Turnbagh, Sarah Peabody, and William A. *Indian Baskets.* West Chester, PA: Schiffer Publishing, 1986.

Wyatt, James C.Y. *The Sumptuous Basket: Chinese Lacquer with Basketry Panels.* San Francisco: China House Gallery and China Institute in America, 1985.

FOLDED BASKETS:

Ekiguchi, Kunio. *Gift Wrapping: Creative Ideas from Japan.* Tokyo: Kodansha International, 1985.

Kondo, Yoko. *Creative Gift Packaging.* Tokyo: Ondorisha Publishers, 1986.

Rossback, Ed. *Baskets As Textile Art.* New York: Van Nostrand Reinhold, 1973.

SHAPING FOR BASKETRY:

LaPlantz, Shereen. *Plaited Basketry: The Woven Form.* Bayside, CA: Press de LaPlantz, 1982.

———. *Plaited Folios.* Bayside, CA: Press de LaPlantz, 1990.

LOOM WEAVING (PATTERNS):

Birrell, Verla. *The Textile Arts.* New York: Schocken Books, 1973.

Davison, Marguerite Porter. *A Handweaver's Pattern Book.* Swarthmore, PA: Self-published, 1944 and 1966.

Held, Shirley E. *Weaving: A Handbook for Fiber Craftsmen.* New York: Holt, Rinehart and Winston, 1973.

Sutton, Ann. *The Structure of Weaving.* Asheville, NC: Lark Books, 1982.

Sources

The following suppliers are gratefully ackowledged for their contributions to this book:

Allen's Basketworks
8624 S.E. Thirteenth
Portland, OR 97202
reed, cane, etc.

Basket Beginnings
P.O. Box 54
Newark, CA 94560-0054
*California basketry materials, exotics,
dyed raffia, reed, and cane*

The Basket Works
77 Mellor Ave.
Baltimore, MD 21228
*ash, oak, poplar, exotics,
reed, cane, books, and tools*

The Caning Shop
926 Gilman St.
Berkeley, CA 94710
reed, cane, and books

Carolina Basketry
2703 Hwy. 70 East
New Bern, NC 28650
*walnut, ash, poplar, hardwood
hoops and handles, reed, and cane*

Cerulean Blue, Ltd
P.O. Box 21168
Seattle, WA 98111-3168
*dyes, with instructions (safety conscious—
provides MSDS on each dye)*

English Basketry Willows
R.F.D. 1, Box 124A
S. New Berlin, NY 13843
willow

G.H. Productions
521 E. Walnut St.
Scottsville, KY 42164
*oak, ash, Nantucket supplies,
reed, and cane*

Irene Gettle
7791 Eighteenth Ave. North
St. Petersburg, FL 33710
*dyed reed, many colors
(Dyeing is a nuisance, and it's toxic;
let her do it for you.)*

Gratiot Lake Basketry
Star Route 1, Box 16
Mohawk, MI 49950
reed, cane, etc.

H.H. Perkins Co.
10 S. Bradley Rd.
Woodbridge, CT 06525
reed, cane, etc.

J. Page Basketry
820 Albee Rd. West
Nokomis, FL 34275
*Florida basketry materials,
reed, cane, and hoops*

Ozark Basketry Supply
P.O. Box 599
Fayetteville, AR 72702
*Ozark basketry materials, reed,
cane, and books*

Royalwood Ltd.
517-RU Woodville Rd.
Mansfield, OH 44907
reed, cane, and books

Vicki Schober Co., Inc.
2363 N. Mayfair Rd.
Milwaukee, WI 53226
microwood and paper

Western Ventures
Route 1, Box 153
Forks, WA 98331
*cedar and Washington
basketry materials*

Metric Equivalency

INCHES	CM
1/8	0.3
1/4	0.6
3/8	1.0
1/2	1.3
5/8	1.6
3/4	1.9
7/8	2.2
1	2.5
1-1/4	3.2
1-3/4	4.4
2	5.1
2-1/2	6.4
3	7.6
3-1/2	8.9
4	10.2
4-1/2	11.4
5	12.7
6	15.2
7	17.8
8	20.3
9	22.9
10	25.4
11	27.9
12	30.5
13	33.0
14	35.6
15	38.1
16	40.6
17	43.2
18	45.7
19	48.3
20	50.8
21	53.3
22	55.9
23	58.4
24	61.0
25	63.5
26	66.0
27	68.6
28	71.1
29	73.7
30	76.2
31	78.7
32	81.3
33	83.8
34	86.4
35	88.9
36	91.4

Index